Bob Dylan in the 2020s

Rough and Rowdy Ways,
Shadow Kingdom,
and all that *Philosophy*

"If you copy from one author, it's plagiarism, but if you copy from many, it's research."

Wilson Mizner

This book has been published for the first time in November 2020, under its French title: *Un album peu tapageur – Rough and Rowdy Ways*.

This is the fourth edition, first edition in English, January 2023 by Tangible Press.

ISBN: 978-1-7375810-2-4

Another book by the same author:

Bob Dylan – Une biographie.

Editions Camion Blanc, December 2021.

Table of contents

Foreword

The first purpose of this essay was the analysis of Bob Dylan's 2020 album, his latest to date, **Rough and Rowdy Ways.** It goes in detail into Bob Dylan's creation process and tries to examine it as a whole as well. It puts forward this idea, that Dylan, to simplify his method, writes his songs by piling up references and quotations, and as a result his songs are way greater than the parts he picked from and added into them.

There have been many analyses of Bob Dylan's songs and writings since the 60's, but it is only since 2001 and *"Love and Theft"* publication, that that peculiar theory has been developed by Dylan critics and fans. The most well-known is Scott Warmuth, who discovered dozens of sources supporting that theory, and now every new Dylan writing is consistently dissected in order to find out its sources, filling up hundreds of web pages.

All those analyses, and some criticisms that ensued them, drew commentaries from their main interested party.

In a press conference, in Rome, on July 23, 2001: "These so-called connoisseurs of Bob Dylan music... I don't feel they know a thing, or have any inkling of who I am and what I'm about. I know they think they do, and yet it's ludicrous, it's humorous, and sad. That such people have spent so much of their time thinking about who? Me? Get a life, please. It's not something any one person should do about another. You're not serving your own life well. You're wasting your life."

On the official web site bobdylan.com, responding to criticisms about his 2011 tour in China, in a sarcastic way: "Everybody knows by now that there's a gazillion books on me either out or coming out in the near future. So I'm encouraging anybody who's ever met me, heard me or even seen me, to get in on the action and scribble their own book. You never know, somebody might have a great book in them."

From an interview with Mikal Gilmore published in Rolling Stone on 27 September 2012: "Oh, yeah, in folk and jazz, quotation is a rich and enriching tradition. That certainly is true. It's true for everybody, but me. I mean, everyone else can do it but not me. There are different rules for me. And as far as Henry Timrod is concerned, have you even heard of him? Who's been reading him lately? And who's pushed him to the forefront? Who's been making you read him? And ask his descendants what they think of the hoopla. And if you think it's so easy to quote him and it can help your work, do it yourself and see how far you can get. Wussies and pussies complain about that stuff. It's an old thing – it's part of the tradition. It goes way back. These are the same people that tried to pin the name Judas on me. Judas, the most hated name in human history! If you think you've been called a bad name, try to work your way out from under that. Yeah, and for what? For playing an electric guitar? As if that is in some kind of way equitable to betraying our Lord and delivering him up to be crucified. All those evil motherfuckers can rot in hell. I'm working within my art form. It's that simple. I work within the rules and limitations of it. There are authoritarian figures that can explain that kind of art form better to you than I can. It's called songwriting. It has to do with melody and rhythm, and then after that, anything goes. You make everything yours. We all do it."

And lately, from an interview with Douglas Brinkley published in the New York times, 12 June 2020: "The names themselves are not solitary. It's the combination of them that adds up to something more than their singular parts. To go too much into detail is irrelevant. The song is like a painting, you can't see it all at once if you're standing too close. The individual pieces are just part of a whole."

Well, whether Bob Dylan likes it or not, those analyses will continue, probably long after his death. Besides, when you really like a painting, you look at it as a whole, then you get closer to watch its details, there's no contradiction between both those outlooks.

Most Bob Dylan songs, especially his newest ones, do not tell a story. Their melody and their lyrics create an atmosphere. They call on several thoughts at the same time. Often times a line, even part of a line, draws from several sources, and it may take several meanings. As it happens, a song meaning may change through time. Greatest valued creations have this peculiarity, their author did not foresee all they implied at the moment they were written.

My ambition is not to deliver the truth about Bob Dylan's songs, but I tried to provide some understanding and shed light on his writing process, and offer assumptions for their deciphering, hoping I would get closer to their real meaning, keeping in mind no one can claim an absolute position in any understanding and interpretation of an artwork.

My choice was to start by analyzing "Murder Most Foul," for it is linked to the other ones, and my opinion is it is the most important song in **Rough and Rowdy Ways**. I dealt with the other songs in the album's order. For analyzing a song's lyrics, I followed their natural reading. If ever a line or several lines are not dealt with, they won't be revisited, allowing for exceptions.

Chapter 12, **Shadow Kingdom**, has been added in later editions, same for commentaries about 2021 and 2022 tours, and about Bob Dylan's latest book, **The Philosophy of Modern Song**.

1 - An Album That Aroused Some Rowdiness

On June 19, 2020, big surprise, **Rough and Rowdy Ways** was released on 2 CDs, first album with original compositions by Bob Dylan in 8 years! Three songs were first released on the internet, to be followed on July 24 by a release on 2 vinyl LP's, delayed by pressing factories unavailability due to the Covid-19 pandemic. The whole album lasts fewer than 71 minutes, so it could have filled only one CD, yet its second CD contains only one song, "Murder Most Foul." It reminds us of the fourth side of the **Blonde on Blonde** album, containing only "Sad Eyed Lady of the Lowlands." Besides black, the vinyl version was issued in limited supply in 3 other colors – olive green, yellow, and gold – sold only by independent record shops.

Recording dates are uncertain, some argued the songs were recorded during 2019 recording sessions, others in 2012 at sessions for **Tempest**, Dylan's previous album of original songs. As far as we know, the sessions took place on January and February 2020, although some of the songs were probably written long before that. "Murder Most Foul" especially is rumored to have been written, and maybe tried out in the studio, at the **Tempest** recording sessions.

The first question that comes to mind is, why did Bob Dylan bother to write, play and release one more album, when he could boast of so many, 38 already, plus live albums, compilations, and outtakes from previous sessions (*The Bootleg Series*). One cannot say he is prone to idleness, knowing he toured constantly since 1988, performing an average of 90 shows a year. In addition, he produced paintings and sculptures, not to mention further volumes of *Chronicles*, that he committed to by contract. Many regarded his 2012 album, **Tempest**, to be his last ever, as if to say his 'last will.' Some Dylan scholars suggested that the album title, **Tempest**, was a clue to it being Bob Dylan's final album, just like *The Tempest* was Shakespeare's final play. The **Rough and Rowdy Ways** release refuted that idea. In his book *The True Performing of It: Bob Dylan and William Shakespeare,* Andrew Muir denied both propositions, showing William Shakespeare did write another play after *The Tempest*. Bob Dylan's 'fans and followers' knew he spent some time in recording studios since 2013, but nobody suspected he wrote music and lyrics for 10 brand new songs. The prospect of not being allowed to play live for a long time was probably one of the reasons for writing them, and in all likelihood, he had a few songs or sketches of songs on hand. We can imagine as well he enjoyed catching off-guard all those who claimed Bob Dylan would rest on his laurels and never write anything of interest now that he received the Nobel Prize. At this moment in time, we can only guess his reasons, maybe we will learn more in the future.

Besides Bob Dylan playing the harp and the guitar – not the piano as he used to in his shows since 2003 – all five members of his 2019 group play on this album: Charlie Sexton on guitar, Donnie Herron on violin, mandolin and steel guitar, Robert Britt on guitar (he took part in **Time Out of Mind** recording sessions), Tony Garnier on bass, and Matt Chamberlain on drums and percussion. A few guests were added: Blake Mills on guitar and harmonium, Benmont Tench on Hammond organ (he played with Bob on the **Shot of Love** album, then in 1986-87 with the Tom Petty group), Alan Pasqua on piano (he played the music for Dylan's speech for his Nobel Prize, and on the 1978 tour), Tommy Rhodes on guitar, and Fiona Apple on piano, on "Murder Most Foul" only. Fiona Apple, Blake Mills and Charlie Sexton sang backing vocals. Chris Shaw, who worked with Bob in 1999 for the track "Things Have Changed," and later for *"Love and Theft"* and *Modern Times* albums, took part in producing and mixing. Blake Mills claimed he took most of the production job, although he was not credited, and published his guitar parts on the internet. Bob asked Robbie Robertson, founding member of his well-known group The Band, who played with him from 1965 to 1974, to play at those sessions, but Robertson was busy with other projects, and personally I do not think it would have been for the better.

The album's sleeve is minimal. It comprises 3 photographs and a list of song titles and musicians, specifying the instruments they played, but only for Dylan's current stage group, not for the other players. There is no detail on the sessions' proceedings. Josh Cheuse was in charge of the design. He started by phoning to the English group The Clash and asking them if they needed a photograph, then he shot photos for the Beastie Boys, and for various magazines, and went to videos and web sites design, and is now Associated Design Director at Sony Music company.

The front sleeve photography has been taken by Ian Berry in 1964 in a London club for black customers, whose window overlooked Cable Street, known for a 1936 riot between fascists and anti-fascists. It was colorized, and so was the inside photography. That front photo shows a couple dancing and a third character looking at the jukebox, which is not obvious, the room being poorly lighted. It has been used before on the front cover of several books and records. The inside sleeve shows figures of Jimmie Rodgers at foreground, with the Carter Family, photographed on June 10, 1931 in Louisville, Kentucky Main Street, at the time they played a few shows together in U.S. center states cities. The Carter Family was a huge influence on Woody Guthrie, and he is well-known for having been Bob Dylan's "only idol." The back photography of President John Fitzgerald Kennedy was taken by a Press Agency, and the above title – *Murder Most Foul* – is in gothic lettering, which omens the album's content, as we shall see later in this book.

A 1929 Jimmie Rodgers song, "My Rough and Rowdy Ways," is the most obvious source of inspiration for that album title. It appeared on several compilations and as the title for a Rodgers album. Bob Dylan removed its possessive, *My*, making it more universal. Notwithstanding Woody Guthrie who used this locution in his *Bound for Glory* novel. Dylan covered Jimmie Rodgers "Muleskinner Blues" in 1962, a recording at Montreal's Finjan club is circulating, where Dylan can be heard yodeling the way Rodgers did. In May 1994 too he covered "My Blue-Eyed Jane," and he wrote laudatory liner notes for that tribute album, *Jimmie Rodgers – A Tribute*, in his distinguished style:

"Jimmie Rodgers of course is one of the guiding lights of the Twentieth Century whose way with song has always been an inspiration to those of us who have followed the path. A blazing star whose sound was and remains the raw essence of individuality in a sea of conformity, par excellence with no equal. Though he is claimed as The Father of Country Music, the title is limiting and deceiving in light of today's country music and he wouldn't have understood it. In his time, he was better known as 'The Singing Brakeman' or 'Blue Yodeler' and hence in some circles, he has come to be known as the 'Man Who Started It All' which is more to the truth for he was a performer of force without precedent with a sound as lonesome and mystical as it was dynamic. He gives hope to the vanquished and humility to the mighty. Indeed, he sings not only among his bawdy, upbeat blues and railroading songs, but also Tin Pan Alley trash and crooner lullabies as well. He makes everything unmistakably his own and does it with piercing charm. Jerry Lee Lewis once said that there are only four stylists – Jimmie, Al Jolson, Hank Williams and himself. Jerry Lee doesn't give out compliments lightly. If we look back far enough, Jimmie may very well be the 'man who started it all' for we have no antecedent to compare him. His refined style, an amalgamation of sources unknown, is too cryptic to pin down. His is a thousand and one voices yet singularly his own.

The artists on this compilation as diverse as ever, all have one thing in common – all have been amazed, moved and enormously affected by Jimmie like no other. Why? Because Jimmie was alive in a way that others were not and are not. His message is all between the lines and he delivers it like nectar that can drill through steel. He gets somehow into the mystery of life and death without saying too much, has some kind of uncanny ability to translate it – he's like the smell of flowers. He stood over there far apart, this is so obvious. No supporting actor in a melodrama or a screw in a machine, not a team player, no old liner or stick in the mud, he is the ring-master general and is as in the Warren Smith ballad, the man who '...held your hand and sang you a song.' What more could he do?

We love the man and we love what he did in the short time he was here and we know that he rose above insur-mountable odds in giving of himself with Herculean effort to achieve it, that he worked against time with a disease that was a quick assignment to the cemetery. We don't salute ourselves in making this record but we point you back there so you can feel it for yourself and see how far off the path we've come. Times change and don't change. The nature of humanity has stayed the same. Jimmie is at the heart of it all with a serious-ness and humor that is befuddling, notwithstanding that infa-mous blue yodel that defies the rational and conjecturing mind. His is the voice in the wilderness of your head...only in turning up the volume can we determine our own destiny."

The album title, **Rough and Rowdy Ways**, has been partly proven, since its release caused a 'rowdy' noise in the media and social networks. It has been hailed by most critics among his 10 best albums, some said his best ever. From Un-cut magazine: "He can still surprise us, this complicated man." And from GQ: "Bob Dylan has released a record that is at once a Rosetta Stone and a monumental work of art." And Mojo: "it's a set of songs that provides inspiration when it's in short supply. Call it a vaccine against culture's shrinking expectations and the subsequent sapping of spirit, or just call it great music." Also Rolling Stone: "Dylan has brilliantly timed his new masterwork, an absolute classic. He is exploring terrain nobody else has reached before – yet he just keeps pushing on into the future." And the Los Angeles Times: "A savage pulp-noir masterpiece." And from Pitchfork web site: "Bob Dylan delivers a gorgeous and meticulous record. It is the rare Dylan album that asks to be understood and comes down to meet its audience. The lyrics are striking."

A small minority rated it as nothing new with poor melodies, but this was a perfunctory judgement that could call for a deeper listen.

Among Bob Dylan's colleagues, talking of "Murder Most Foul," Neil Young wrote on his web site: "This song is a masterpiece. It's history told through a radio station, you are here, you are there. Bob's voice is transcendent as he tells our tale in a way only he could. This is a 'don't miss' for any fan of great music and art." Nick Cave added: "It is a perplexing but beautiful song and, like many people, I have been extremely moved by it. Dylan's relentless cascade of song references points to our potential as human beings to create beautiful things, even in the face of our own capacity for malevolence. 'Murder Most Foul' reminds us that all is not lost, as the song itself becomes a lifeline thrown into our current predicament." And Iggy Pop: "***Rough and Rowdy Ways*** is just the album of the year for me that had the depth. His voice just gets better for me."

The album debuted at No. 1 on Billboard's Top Rock Albums and Americana/Folk albums charts, and made No. 1 in the UK chart, and in 9 other European charts. Dylan topped Billboard's Artist 100 chart on July 4, 2020, to become the "top musical act in the U.S." for the first time in his career.

2 - Murder Most Foul

"Murder Most Foul" was the first title to appear on the internet, debuting on March 27, 2020. It is the album's most remarkable song. For one thing it is very long, seventeen minutes, a record even for Bob Dylan – even though a rumored version of "Highlands" is said to last nineteen minutes – furthermore it has an amazing number of references. This essay will try to discover them all, but most likely a few will stay hidden, and only time may reveal them, possibly. Its publication was illustrated with a John Fitzgerald Kennedy photograph, and its most obvious topic is the killing of President Kennedy, which took place on November 22, 1963 in Dallas, Texas.

The internet release came with a few words by Bob Dylan:

"Greetings to my fans and followers with gratitude for all your support and loyalty across the years. This is an unreleased song we recorded a while back that you might find interesting. Stay safe, stay observant and may God be with you."

That word *observant*, referring to Judaism – Bob Dylan's first faith – describes someone who strictly obeys religious laws, found in the Hebrew Bible and holy books. Personally, I do not think Bob Dylan would mean that, rather he is giving advice fit for the pandemic time. He knows the New

Testament, and Mark (13:33): "Take ye heed, watch and pray: for ye know not when the time is."

These 3 words *'Murder Most Foul'* appear in the William Shakespeare play *Hamlet*, act I, scene 5, lines 27 and 28. The ghost of Hamlet's father tells his son about his death at his brother's hand. Hamlet is appalled at the revelation that his father had been murdered, and his father's ghost tells him that as he slept in his garden, a villain poured poison into his ear – the very villain who now wears his crown, his brother Claudius:

Murder most foul as in the best it is
But this most foul, strange and unnatural

The *unnatural* word may refer to the Catholic religion, for it says a regicide trespasses against God and the nature of things, and as a matter of fact J. F. Kennedy was a Catholic.

Hamlet's tragedy has previously been referenced by Bob Dylan in "Desolation Row," last song from **Highway 61 Revisited** album, released in 1965. Its fourth verse tells us of Ophelia, Polonius's daughter: "Now Ophelia, she's 'neath the window, for her I feel so afraid." According to Shakespeare authority Andrew Muir, and Dylan specialist as well, the latter was "nourished" with Shakespeare's language through immersing in Appalachian ballads in the early 1960s, as the vocabulary used by the first people coming from England to what would become the United States of America had been saved in them.

"Murder Most Foul" appeared as soon as November 26, 1963, 4 days after the attack, as an article title in an American East Coast newspaper, The Hartford Courant, under the pen of Walter Lippmann, a journalist and commentator influent in politics. The article concerns the recent assassination and calls for "finding a consensus among our divided and angry people." In his 1922 book, *Public Opinion*, Lippmann elaborated on this idea: that the complexity of the contemporaneous world and the multiplicity of information prevent the vast majority of citizens from making a just opinion about issues which they are confronted, and that a class of professional advisers should propose analyses to the governments, who, in their turn, use the 'art of persuasion' to inform the public about the decisions and circumstances affecting them. He named that process the 'manufacture of consent.' Dylan was in the same place as Lippmann at least once, in July 1970, when they both received awards from Princeton University, but there is no evidence they spoke together.

That same title had been used for a film, based on an Agatha Christie novel, *Mrs. McGinty's Dead*. The book was released in 1952, and it features detective Hercule Poirot, whereas the 1964 movie is a Miss Marple story, her third one after "Murder, She Said" and "Murder at the Gallop." Agatha Christie expressed to her publisher her opposition to that title that bore no relation to her novel. The plot starts with Margaret McGinty, a barmaid and former actress, found hanged, and her lodger, caught at the scene, seeming plainly guilty. Everyone believes it to be an open-and-shut case except for Miss Marple, who delves into the case and manages to unmask the killer. Allmovie site gives the film a 4.5 rating.

That very title has also been used for several books, as well as a detective periodical, and a TV series. British attorney Stanley J. Marks' 1967 book, particularly, asks in its subtitle '975 questions and answers' about 'The Conspiracy That Murdered President Kennedy.' He takes a close look at official investigative conclusions following J. F. Kennedy's assassination, and infers that the Warren Commission removed important evidences and neglected questioning essential witnesses. In his book's penultimate chapter, he claims the Commission discovered a conspiracy, contrary to what it says in its report, and its work had been botched. Then Marks adds a remark that no other commentator raised at the time, related to Dylan's song: he writes that, because of the lack of confidence and incredulity the Warren report aroused, cynicism took hold of the general public, and it does not bode well of the American nation's future, for a nation whose moral fiber has been breached and smashed to pieces cannot live long. Although we cannot say if Dylan read this book, we do know he is an avid and curious reader, and that Marks' statement fits in with "Murder Most Foul"'s overall meaning, and maybe the whole album's.

We will come to that, but for the time being here is a detailed explanation of the references within that song.

1	'Twas a dark day in Dallas, November '63
2	A day that will live on in infamy
3	President Kennedy was a-ridin' high
4	A good day to be livin' and a good day to die
5	Being led to the slaughter like a sacrificial lamb
6	He said, "Wait a minute, boys, you know who I am?"
7	"Of course we do, we know who you are!"
8	Then they blew off his head when he was still in the car
9	Shot down like a dog in broad daylight
10	Was a matter of timing and the timing was right
11	"You got unpaid debts, we've come to collect
12	We're gonna kill you with hatred and without any respect
13	We'll mock you and shock you and we'll grin in your face
14	We've already got someone here to take your place"
15	The day they blew out the brains of the king
16	Thousands were watching, no one saw a thing
17	It happened so quickly, so quick, by surprise
18	Right there in front of everyone's eyes
19	Greatest magic trick ever under the sun
20	Perfectly executed, skillfully done
21	Wolfman, oh Wolfman, oh Wolfman howl
22	Rub-a-dub-dub, it's a Murder Most Foul

The way Dylan starts this song, with "'Twas" (archaic contraction of 'It was'), is further evidence if needed that he did not forget his folk influences. That locution can be found at the beginning of many traditional tunes, and in Dylan's songs as well ("John Wesley Harding," "Shelter from the Storm," etc.)

First line is a Tommy Durden song title, "Dark Day in Dallas," but this 'dark day' should be taken figuratively, for, according to all witnesses, the day of November 22, 1963, was sunny in Dallas, Texas. Tommy Durden's main claim to fame is his co-signature with Elvis Presley (and Mae Axton), on the well-known "Heartbreak Hotel."

The "day that will live on in infamy" is a near quotation from the "Infamy Speech," delivered by President Franklin Delano Roosevelt, the day after the Pearl Harbor attack by the Empire of Japan, on December 7, 1941. Soon after the speech, Congress almost unanimously declared war against Japan. In January 1968 – at the Woody Guthrie tribute following his death – Dylan performed a Woody song praising this president, speaking to his wife, "Dear Mrs. Roosevelt," and there is good reason to think he believes in the song's lyrics: "This world was lucky to see him [President Roosevelt] born."

Third line may be interpreted in various ways. In "That's Life," Frank Sinatra sings: "You're ridin' high in April, Shot down in May." Dylan may have thought of this song, although the dates do not match, and both songs do not end the same way. Also, Cole Porter wrote the song "Ridin' High" for his musical *Red, Hot and Blue*, in 1936.

President Kennedy was riding high, it could simply mean his plane was flying high, or it could allude to his habit of taking medicines – JFK's health was uncertain, and he was well-known for taking miscellaneous drugs for his support – it could also mean he was well-liked, his popularity reached the heights, or else it could mean he had an intellectual level and a vision way beyond most of the previous presidents. Lastly that word, 'riding', may be used for any means of transportation, and the presidential limousine rear seat was higher than the driver's seat, the president was high above, which is important for explaining the bullets trajectory, we will talk of that later.

"A good day to die" is a phrase historically associated with certain Native American cultures. Legend has it that Lieutenant-Colonel George Armstrong Custer said it before the Battle of Little Bighorn, in June 1876, where he got killed and the American army was defeated by the Lakota, Northern Cheyenne, and Arapaho coalition. This was known as *Custer's Last Stand*. This line has also been described as the ending of a Lakota Sioux prayer. In the film *Little Big Man*, tribe leader Old Lodge Skins, accompanied by Jack Crabb (Dustin Hoffman) says it before he decides to end his life, but it begins to rain and he finally stays alive. The 1998 film *Smoke Signals* plays with it by putting it in other situations.

Line 5, "sacrificial lamb" obviously refers to the Bible scene where Abraham is asked to sacrifice his son. More particularly, one might think President Kennedy sacrificed himself by promoting racial equality in the U.S., and peace abroad. When he died, there were 13,000 soldiers in Vietnam, and Lyndon B. Johnson, who replaced him, raised this number to half a million.

In line 6, "Wait a minute, boys" had been used in another Bob Dylan song, "Hurricane." It is a first occurrence of self-quotation.

In line 7, Dylan plays a little trick on The Beatles, adapting a line from the well-known McCartney-Lennon song "A Day in the Life," from *Sergeant Pepper's Lonely Hearts Club Band* album: "He blew his mind out in a car."

Line 9 alludes to the novel *To Kill a Mockingbird*, written in 1960 by Harper Lee. In it, Atticus Finch is asked to shoot down a rabid dog in broad daylight, although it is not his job. He did not want to kill the dog, but he felt it his duty to protect the town. Actually the dog represents racial prejudice.

"You got unpaid debts" alludes to the Kennedy clan links with the mafia, which is rumored to have bought votes for the 1960 presidential election.

"We've already got someone here to take your place" refers of course to Vice-President Lyndon B. Johnson, who, following some theories, was informed of what was going to happen. Some even suggested he was part of it.

Line 15 refers to the president as "the king." It alludes to the murdered king in Hamlet, whose ghost cries out "Murder most foul!"

"Thousands were watching, no one saw a thing": Dylan takes liberties with the real facts, as the presidential parade was partly filmed for television, but not the assassination. Many people were present along the way, but only a few hundreds at the assassination place.

In this first verse, Dylan makes frequent use of pronouns 'they' and 'we', telling us of a conspiracy, not a lone killer. On the other hand, we cannot say if the narrator talks of his own point of view, or takes that of a conspiracy theories commentator.

"Greatest magic trick ever under the sun" is from the French 1968 book, *L'Amérique brûle* (America is Burning, released in English as *Farewell America: The Plot to Kill JFK*), written by James Hepburn. The authors (James Hepburn is a pseudonym) conducted clandestine research among KGB and Interpol agents and French petroleum espionage specialists and relied on a rare, unmodified print of the famed Zapruder film (more later). The book defends the Kennedys and their ideals, and seeks to dismiss the 'lone gunman' theory of JFK's assassination. "Executed," in line 20, should clearly be taken as a double meaning.

At the end of the first verse, Dylan talks of disc-jockey Wolfman Jack, who made himself famous thanks to his rocky voice and his changes of appearance, entailing his nickname of Wolfman or Werewolf. He had a role in the film *American Graffiti*, on which he got a share of the royalties, which assured him a lifetime income. He also took part in various radio and television programs, more importantly from 1962 to 1964 from a Mexican radio, XERF, where he took in a signature *howl*, inspired by the bluesman Howlin' Wolf, and another DJ, Alan Freed, who called himself the "Moon Dog" after Moondog, an experimental street musician in New-York. It is highly likely Dylan listened to those programs, since that radio station broadcast very far and he loved listening to the radio. Several artists alluded to this disc-jockey – The Doors in "The WASP (Texas Radio and the Big Beat)," Todd Rundgren on the album *Something/Anything?*, The Grateful Dead in "Ramble On Rose" – or else had him take part in their songs. He was rumored to be a CIA agent, and as such knew more about some events than the average American.

The name *Wolfman* might as well refer to Wolfgang Mozart, who was a well-known freemason, as there are other masonic references in that song.

The penultimate line quotes *Howl*, Allen Ginsberg's poem. Ginsberg was Dylan's friend from their first meeting, in 1964, until his death in 1997. He was invited on the 1975 tour, *Rolling Thunder Revue*, and recorded with Dylan in 1971. This poem is famous for its first lines: "I saw the best minds of my generation destroyed by madness, starving hysterical naked," often quoted or parodied in American literature.

Dylan ends the verse with a childish refrain, as if he warned his listener not to take too seriously his grownup stories. Or else it is a pun with the slang "rub out," as in Raymond Chandler's story *Trouble Is My Business*: "somebody rubbed him out this afternoon with a twenty-two." A song named "Rub a Dub Dub" can also be found on a 2001 tribute to Wolfman Jack record: *Wolfman Jack's Graffiti Gold Goofy Greats*.

22	Hush, little children, you'll soon understand
23	The Beatles are coming, they're gonna hold your hand
24	Slide down the banister, go get your coat
25	"Ferry 'cross the Mersey" and go for the throat
26	There's three bums comin' all dressed in rags
27	Pick up the pieces and lower the flags
28	I'm going to Woodstock, it's the Aquarian Age
29	Then I'll go over to Altamont and sit near the stage
30	Put your head out the window, let the good times roll
31	There's a party going on behind the Grassy Knoll
32	Stack up the bricks and pour the cement
33	Don't say Dallas doesn't love you, Mr. President
34	Put your foot in the tank and step on the gas
35	Try to make it to the Triple Underpass
36	Blackface singer, whiteface clown
37	Better not show your faces after the sun goes down
38	I'm in the red-light district like a cop on the beat
39	Living in a nightmare on Elm Street
40	When you're down on Deep Ellum, put your money in your shoe
41	Don't ask what your country can do for you
42	Cash on the barrelhead, money to burn
43	Dealey Plaza, make a left-hand turn
44	I'm going down to the crossroads, gonna flag a ride
45	That's the place where Faith, Hope and Charity died
46	Shoot him while he runs, boy, shoot him while you can
47	See if you can shoot The Invisible Man

48	Goodbye, Charlie, goodbye Uncle Sam!
49	Frankly, Miss Scarlett, I don't give a damn
50	What is the truth, and where did it go?
51	Ask Oswald and Ruby, they oughta know
52	"Shut your mouth," says the wise old owl
53	Business is business, and it's a Murder Most Foul

First verse exposed the context, references were based on American history. Second verse continued addressing the children, the "Wise Old Owl" (line 52) is watching and telling us what he is seeing, in short sentences like orders and advices.

Dylan quotes again The Beatles, their big 1964 hit "I Want to Hold Your Hand," that he belittled for its simplistic lyrics, before he admitted its melody and harmonies encouraged him to go from Folk to Rock. At first Dylan believed the song said "When I touch you I get high," when the real lyrics were "I can't hide." He found that out from John Lennon's mouth, when he met The Beatles, on August 28, 1964 at the Delmonico hotel in New York.

Line 24 mentions Guy Banister's name. He was an FBI agent, Freemason and member of the John Birch Society. This far-right political group opposed the 1960s Civil Rights Movement and claimed the Movement had communists in important positions. Bob Dylan made fun of it in his 1962 song "Talkin' John Birch Society Blues." Banister was alleged to be a munitions supplier for the Bay of Pigs Invasion in 1961. He worked as a private investigator with David Ferrie, quoted in line 25. Dylan plays on words and refers in this line to the Gerry & The Pacemakers song, "Ferry Cross the Mersey" too. Banister and Ferrie were suspected to have taken part in the president's killing. Jim Garrison, the district attorney of New Orleans, investigated JFK's assassination. He interviewed Jack Martin, who knew both men, and Martin told him Ferrie met several times with Lee Harvey Oswald, JFK's murderer. In 1979, the House Select Committee on Assassinations stated that available records "lent substantial credence to the possibility that Oswald and Ferrie had been involved in the same [Civil Air Patrol] C.A.P. unit during the same period of time." Banister died in 1964, and Ferrie in 1967, less than a week after a New Orleans newspaper broke the story of Garrison's investigation. Garrison believed that Banister, Ferrie, and a third guy named Clay Shaw had conspired to set up Oswald as a patsy in JFK's assassination.

Line 26 alludes to another conspiracy theory, the three tramps. Dallas-area newspaper photographs show three men under police escort near the Texas School Book Depository, shortly after the assassination. This led to construct various scenarios, until in 1992 a journalist got access to the Dallas Police Department arrest records and found out the three men were "taken off a boxcar in the railroad yards right after President Kennedy was shot," and revealed no new information about the assassination, then they were released four days later.

In lines 28 and 29, Dylan summarizes the peak and letdown of the hippie dream, from the age of Aquarius, that was pictured on the Woodstock festival first poster, to the Altamont concert, which ended with three dead just in front of the stage, and struck a fatal blow to the Sixties. Dylan foresaw from the beginning that the hippie movement was only an illusion and declined to play at the Woodstock festival, even though it was planned to take place very near his home at the time.

"Put your head out the window" quotes "The Ballad of Casey Jones," a traditional telling the story of a train driver who gave his life to avoid a collision, that has been sung by Pete Seeger, The Golden Gate Quartet, Bing Crosby, and others.

"Let the Good Times Roll" is a well-known tune sung by Louis Jordan in 1946, and Shirley and Lee in 1956, two versions Dylan has known for a long time, without being carried away. It is a documentary film too, as a Rock'n'Roll show, with Chuck Berry, Bo Diddley, Fats Domino, Little Richard (Robert Zimmerman's favorite musician when in college), and others. From the same period, "There's a Party Going On" was sung by Wanda Jackson, a Rock'n'Roll pioneer woman. Next on the same line (31), the narrator brings another element of conspiracy, the Grassy Knoll where a fourth shot would have been fired, not by Lee Oswald.

The "cement" in line 32 alludes to the theory of Freemason rites for the assassination. In the same way, in line 81 the narrator says he has seen the Zapruder film "thirty-three times," but it should not be taken literally, this number refers to the theory elaborated in the book *King-Kill 33°*. The thirty-third degree is the highest one in the Ancient and Accepted Scottish Rite of Freemasonry, founded in 1801 in the U.S.

While riding in the car with President Kennedy, Nellie Connally, Governor of Texas' wife, told President Kennedy, "Mr. President, you can't say Dallas doesn't love you," which President Kennedy acknowledged by saying "No, you certainly can't." Within a few seconds, she heard the first gunshot aimed at the president. Those close to the president had reasons for being concerned about the kind of reception he would get in Dallas, since businessmen paid for a full page in Dallas' main newspaper lambasting his politics. Ms. Connally's sentence echoes to a sarcastic phrase supposedly asked to President Abraham Lincoln's wife, right after his assassination while attending a theater play: "Other than that, how was the play, Mrs. Lincoln?"

"Put your foot in the tank" quotes from Chuck Berry's song "You Can't Catch Me," and this title meaning is related to the topic of Dylan's song. The second part of this line (34), "step on the gas," is a pun between "gas" and "grass", which alludes to the Grassy Knoll three lines above, and to marijuana too. At the same time, it is a common English sign: "Don't step on the grass."

For those who do not know Dallas, Texas, the Triple Underpass (line 35) is a crossroad with an underground passage, located close to Dealey Plaza, where the assassination took place. This Plaza is a small square in the Dallas historic center. The presidential limousine turned left from Houston Street into Elm Street, as indicated in line 43. In 1964, Dylan did a road trip with two friends: Victor Maimudes who was his road manager in the 1960s and 1980s, and Paul Clayton who was an American folksinger and folklorist prominent in the folk music revival of the 1950s and 1960s. Bob took the melody and a few lines from his song "Who's Gonna Buy You Ribbons When I'm Gone?" for his song "Don't Think Twice, It's All Right," and learned from him the song "Gotta Travel On," among others. They went to Dallas to see Dealey Plaza. The story says they asked their way to this place and no one would answer them. When they found it at last, they repeated the presidential limousine route, stopping frequently to remember what happened at each place.

In the next line, Dylan evokes the blackface singers, racist shows that lasted in the U.S. until the middle of the twentieth century. Dylan referred to these kinds of shows for the first time in his 1969 song "Minstrel Boy," played at his Isle of Wight show, and much more in his 2001 album *"Love and Theft"*, whose title he took from the Eric Lott book about minstrel shows and their interaction between black and white people.

Line 37, "After the Sun Goes Down" is a song by Keven "Dino" Conner, member of the R'n'B group H-Town, founded in 1990. A rather unexpected reference coming from Dylan, but Rythm'n'Blues was known to be his favorite music as a teenager, and even if this kind of music has changed significantly, one may think he has fun hearing the way this group handles words. This line alludes to the curfew for black people: in some towns, they were not allowed to walk in the street at night, that is why Robert Johnson is trying to "flag a ride" at the crossroad. See below.

Line 38 last word, 'beat', brings to mind the poets of the literary movement that substantially influenced Bob Dylan, particularly the Jack Kerouac and Allen Ginsberg figures. It may also refer to the Eric Andersen piece, "Beat Avenue." Eric Andersen was part of the Folk renaissance movement, as was Bob Dylan. They played and hung out at the same places in Greenwich Village. In 1970 Dylan covered his song "Thirsty Boots," released in 2013 in *The Bootleg Series Vol. 10: Another Self Portrait (1969–1971)*. In 2003 Andersen released his album *Beat Avenue*, whose twenty-six-minute title song relates his experiences in the San Francisco Beat community on the day of President Kennedy's assassination.

Dallas' criminal quarter, Deep Ellum, appears in lines 39 and 40. From the twenties to the sixties, it was one of the most disreputable areas in the U.S. All sorts of crimes and misdemeanors happened there, from illegal gambling to drug dealing to selling guns, and murders were common. It was a musician's hideout – Leadbelly, Robert Johnson, Blind Lemon Jefferson, Bessie Smith – and they wrote songs about this area. The oldest known was "Deep Elm Blues," sung by the group Lone Star Cowboys. Dylan sang it in 1962, titled "Deep Ellum Blues," and it had been covered by The Grateful Dead, who played with Dylan in 1987. "Put your money in your shoe" in line 40 is from this song, and Dylan quoted this line in his 2015 *MusiCares* speech. In the 1980s and 1990s, Deep Ellum became a key site for the U.S. artistic scene, and punk group Dead *Kennedys* played often in its clubs. This name was used as well for the media franchise *A Nightmare on Elm Street*, beginning in 1984 with the so titled film and including eight other films and various media. Ronee Blakley, whom Dylan recruited for his Rolling Thunder Revue tour, played a role in the 1984 film.

Line 41, Dylan refers to a sentence from JFK's inaugural speech on January 20, 1961: "And so, my fellow Americans: ask not what your country can do for you – ask what you can do for your country. My fellow citizens of the world: ask not what America will do for you, but what together we can do for the freedom of man." These words are engraved on JFK's tombstone in Arlington cemetery. The speech as a whole was about the state of the world during the Cold War, and the difficulties in American society, and expressed an optimistic faith in the American people, who should make the best of the present situation.

Then the narrator goes back to the assassination, quoting from a Louvin Brothers song, "Cash on the Barrel Head." A colloquial way of saying 'pay in full', which recalls the "unpaid debts" from first verse. "Money to Burn" was a hit for Country singer George Jones.

The "crossroads" allude to the Robert Johnson song, whose legend says he met the devil at a crossroad and sold him his soul against the gift of playing the guitar as a virtuoso. "Flag a ride" in the same line (44) is obviously a quotation from this song, but it is also a reminder of the pennants bedecking the presidential automobile, the American flag and the presidency flag.

After the devil, the song refers to Catholicism: Faith, Hope and Charity (or Love) are the three theological virtues. They first appeared as such in St. Paul's first letter to the Thessalonians 1:3 and First Epistle to the Corinthians, chapter 13. As we all know, Bob Dylan was raised in the Jewish faith, but he often quoted the New Testament in his songs, and the Kennedy family is Catholic, actually JFK was the first Catholic president of the U.S.A. For many, JFK embodied these virtues which "died" at the crossroad where the killing took place, and it has been a spiritual crossroad as well in the history of the U.S.

In line 46, "Shoot him while he runs" is a near quote from Junior Walker's song, "Shotgun," for which he received a Grammy Award nomination. He was an American saxophonist and vocalist who recorded for Motown during the 1960s. He also performed as a session and live-performing saxophonist with the band Foreigner during the 1980s. JFK was sitting still in his seat when he got killed, so 'run' could be understood in this context as running for president.

JFK could not be an "Invisible Man" (line 47), nor could Bob Dylan who was afraid of getting shot as soon as 1964, and much more after John Lennon's killing in 1980. These words bring to mind the famous H. G. Wells novel, but allude most probably to Ralph Ellison's book with a similar title. This book addresses many of the social and intellectual issues faced by African Americans in the early twentieth century, as well as issues of individuality and personal identity. It won the U.S. National Book Award for Fiction in 1953, making Ellison the first African American writer to win the award. According to The New York Times, Barack Obama modeled his 1995 memoir *Dreams from My Father* on Ellison's novel. The narrator in *Invisible Man* says, "I am not complaining, nor am I protesting either," signaling the break from the usual protest novel, the kind written by previous African American writers who wrote only for social protest. This stance echoes Dylan saying he never wanted to be a "protest-singer."

Ralph Ellison then published a collection of short stories, *Shadow and Act*. Its title is based on the fifth verse of *Hollow Men*, a poem written by T. S. Eliot:

> Between the idea
> And the reality
> Between the motion
> And the act
> Falls the Shadow

It is an indirect link to the picture of *The Shadow* for Dylan's song "False Prophet" (cf. chapter 4). Moreover, that same poem ends with a few lines which appears to be a lyric change of "Here We Go Round the Mulberry Bush" nursery rhyme:

> This is the way the world ends
> Not with a bang but a whimper

If it is not going too far, Dylan could have written those lines, for in many of his song lyrics resonate with the end of the world – "Hard Rain," "Masters of War," "Senor," "Are You Ready," "When He Returns," "Can't Wait," "Cross the Green Mountain," "Nettie Moore," "Scarlet Town," and more.

Goodbye Charlie (line 48) is a 1964 Vincente Minelli film, with Tony Curtis, but it actually refers to the Vietnam War, as "Charlie" was a nickname American soldiers gave to the communist fighters, using Viet Cong initials in the ICAO spelling alphabet (Victor Charlie, then Charlie only). So, the Charlie's did say goodbye to America, to Uncle Sam. "Charlie Don't Surf" is a famous line in the film *Apocalypse Now*, which English punk group The Clash took over as a song title in their third album, *Sandinista*. Additionally, 'Mr. Charlie' was what the black man called the white man. It may be heard in old blues songs, and in James Baldwin's play, *Blues for Mr. Charlie*. This play is dedicated to the memory of Medgar Evers, his widow and children, and to the memory of the dead children of Birmingham. It is loosely based on the Emmett Till murder that occurred in Mississippi, before the Civil Rights Movement began. Bob Dylan wrote a song about Medgar Evers ("Only a Pawn in Their Game") and one about Emmett Till.

"Frankly, my dear, I don't give a damn" is a line from the 1939 film *Gone with the Wind*, spoken by Rhett Butler (Clark Gable), as his last words to Scarlett O'Hara (Vivien Leigh), in response to her tearful question: "Where shall I go?

What shall I do?". The film has been criticized by black commentators since its release for its depiction of black people and "whitewashing" of the issue of slavery. In June 2022 – three months after the "Murder Most Foul" release – the film was removed from HBO Max amid the George Floyd murder protests, until it returned to the streaming service preceded by a statement about its historical context.

Lines 50 and 51 remind us no one knows the truth about what happened in Dallas on November 22, 1963, only Oswald and his killer Jack Ruby could help, had they been still alive.

The narrator ends again the verse with a childish line, like the first verse. So said the Wise Old Owl:

> The more he heard, the less he spoke
> The less he spoke, the more he heard
> O, if men were all like that wise bird
> And grownups too should take note.

54	Tommy, can you hear me? I'm "The Acid Queen"
55	I'm riding in a long, black Lincoln limousine
56	Ridin' in the backseat next to my wife
57	Headed straight on into the afterlife
58	I'm leaning to the left, I got my head in her lap
59	Oh Lord, I've been led into some kind of a trap
60	Well, we ask no quarter, and no quarter do we give
61	We're right down the street, from the street where you live
62	They mutilated his body and they took out his brain
63	What more could they do? They piled on the pain
64	But his soul was not there where it was supposed to be at
65	For the last fifty years they've been searchin' for that
66	Freedom, oh freedom, freedom over me
67	I hate to tell you, mister, but only dead men are free

68	Send me some loving tell me no lie
69	Throw the gun in the gutter and walk on by
70	Wake up, Little Suzie, let's go for a drive
71	Cross the Trinity River, let's keep hope alive
72	Turn the radio on, don't touch the dial
73	Parkland Hospital's only six more miles
74	You got me Dizzy, Miss Lizzy, you filled me with lead
75	That magic bullet of yours has gone to my head
76	I'm just a patsy like Patsy Cline
77	I never shot anyone from in front or behind
78	Got blood in my eye, got blood in my ear
79	I'm never gonna make it to the New Frontier
80	Zapruder's film I've seen that before
81	Seen it thirty-three times, maybe more
82	It's vile and deceitful, it's cruel and it's mean
83	Ugliest thing that you ever have seen
84	They killed him once and they killed him twice
85	Killed him like a human sacrifice
86	The day that they killed him, someone said to me, "Son
87	The age of the Anti-Christ has just only begun"
88	Air Force One coming in through the gate
89	Johnson sworn in at two thirty-eight
90	Let me know when you decide to throw in the towel
91	It is what it is, and it's Murder Most Foul

Third verse goes on with the assassination tale as seen by its protagonists. At the beginning we take the president's place, then the narrator asks the disc-jockey to play for him, all kinds of music more or less related to the event, a musical history of the U.S. overview.

Dylan starts by quoting two Who songs, "Tommy, Can You Hear Me" and "Acid Queen." This alludes to acid, or LSD, and the "Acid Queen" might be Mary Pinchot Meyer. She supposedly was JFK's lover, who talked to Timothy Leary, to persuade him to organize LSD taking sessions with important people, including the president, hoping they realize it would be pure madness to engage in a nuclear war – LSD was legal in the U.S. until October 1968. In his memoirs, Leary recalled he got a phone call from this woman after the assassination, suggesting it was a staged event. She was killed by two gunshots while walking along a canal, three weeks after the Warren Commission report publication.

President Kennedy's official car was a Lincoln Cabriolet limousine, model 74A, code name for secret services SS-100-X. Following his death, it was upgraded with an armor-plating and other enhancements, which increased significantly its value, to the extent that it was used until 1977. This type of car is often associated with funerals. Southern rocker Jerry Lee Lewis wrote a song entitled "Lincoln Limousine," whose explicit topic was JFK's assassination. Also, an Elvis Presley song, "Long Black Limousine" tells of a tragic accident. As noticed by dylanologue Michael Gray, Dylan insists on the word *Lincoln*, who is precisely the first murdered American president.

Line 58, "I'm leaning to the left," may refer to the president's political positioning, as well as his body position towards his wife, after the gunshots.

Line 60, "No Quarter" is a pirate phrase meaning "no mercy," and a well-known track from English group Led Zeppelin.

Line 61 is similar to "On the Street Where You Live," a song from the musical comedy *My Fair Lady*. It was sung by Nat King Cole, Dean Martin, Vic Damone, and others. As pointed out by Michael Gray, Bob Dylan already borrowed lines from this song in his own "The Man in Me," almost quoting it exactly, in words and tune.

Line 62, "They mutilated his body and they took out his brain": JFK's brain was removed during autopsy, and he himself was *taken out* of this world.

Line 66, "Oh Freedom" is a post-Civil War African-American freedom song. It is often associated with the Civil Rights Movement, with Odetta, and with Joan Baez, who performed the song at the 1963 March on Washington, Bob Dylan was there too.

Line 67, Country singer Larry Butler wrote in 1997 a piece entitled "Only the Dead Are Free." Willie Nelson sang it.

"Send Me Some Lovin'" had been recorded in 1956 by Little Richard, and covered by many artists: Sam Cooke, Dean Martin, Stevie Wonder, Otis Redding, Gene Vincent, John Lennon, and others. This line might allude to JFK's love affairs.

Line 69, "Walk on By" had been written by Burt Bacharach and Hal David for Dionne Warwick in 1963, and was recorded at the same studio session that produced the famous song "Anyone Who Had a Heart." As before, this advice to the president should be taken figuratively.

"Wake Up Little Susie" is a popular song written by Felice and Boudleaux Bryant and published in 1957. The song is best known in a recording by the Everly Brothers. It was banned from Boston radio stations for it tells how a teenage couple fell asleep at the drive-in and did not wake up until 4 am, well after the curfew. The name Susie reminds us of Suze Rotolo who was young Dylan's girlfriend.

Lines 71 and 73, The Trinity River and Parkland hospital are located near the site of the assassination. The hospital, where they brought the dying president, is actually around nine miles from Dealey Plaza, Dylan may have written "six miles" for his listeners to think of the Hank Williams song, "Six More Miles to the Graveyard." Another reason might be that the murder weapon was found at the *sixth* floor in the Texas School Book Depository, a building located at 411 Elm Street, where Oswald had a temporary job.

Line 71, "Keep hope alive" has been made famous as a slogan from Reverend and black leader Jesse Jackson, he said it specifically to refer Martin Luther King's death.

Line 72, "Don't touch the dial," so said radio disc-jockeys before the advertisements, at a time when everybody listened to the radio, for fear they changed the station to avoid the ads.

Line 74, "Dizzy Miss Lizzy" is a song composed and performed by Larry Williams in 1958, then covered and popu-larized by The Beatles in 1965, in their album *Help!* "You filled me with lead" means shooting with bullets in slang and could be word-play: lead is heavy and "dizzy" means lightheaded.

"Magic bullet" (line 75) refers to Dr. Paul Ehrlich's term for a medicine so potent it cures an ailment as if by magic, without deleterious side effects. His story is told in the 1940 film *Dr. Ehrlich's Magic Bullet*, that had problems with the Motion Pic-ture Production Code because the ailment was syphilis, a taboo topic, and because Ehrlich was Jewish. The use of the words "magic bullet" here is ironic as it killed, not cured.

A Warren Commission senator affirmed that one "magic bullet" caused all the non-fatal wounds to President John Kennedy and Governor John Connally, which adds up to seven entry/exit wounds in both men. This theory is disputed, for the course of the bullet would have been highly unlikely, nearly impossible, to cause all those injuries. At least two bullets would have been needed to make them. Several shots were suspected, even several shooters. Governor Connally, who was in front of President Kennedy in the car, always maintained he was shot by another bullet than the one that hit the president, but the final report found "persuasive evidence from the experts" for the single-bullet theory, and that all members of the Commission had no doubt that all shots were fired from the sixth-floor window of the Depository building.

"I'm just a patsy" is a quotation from Lee Harvey Oswald denying the murder of President John F. Kennedy. Dylan makes a pun with the Country singer Patsy Cline's name. He covered the song "You Belong to Me," sung by Patsy Cline in 1952, for his 1992 album *Good as I Been to You*, but it was shelved and finally released on the Oliver Stone *Natural Born Killers* soundtrack. The Canadian 2005 film *C.R.A.Z.Y.* soundtrack includes Patsy Cline and Charles Aznavour. We know Dylan likes Aznavour and is a movie buff, so maybe that's why he recorded that Patsy Cline track...

"I've Got Blood in My Eyes for You" (line 78) is a title sung by the Mississippi Sheiks, covered by Dylan in 1993 in his album *World Gone Wrong*.

The term New Frontier (line 79) was used by Democratic presidential candidate John F. Kennedy in his acceptance speech in the 1960 U. S. presidential election to the Democratic National Convention: "We stand today on the edge of a New Frontier – the frontier of the 1960s, the frontier of unknown opportunities and perils, the frontier of unfilled hopes and unfilled threats. ... Beyond that frontier are uncharted areas of science and space, unsolved problems of peace and war, unconquered problems of ignorance and prejudice, unanswered questions of poverty and surplus." "New Frontier" has also been sung by Donald Fagen, former singer of Steely Dan, and Bob Dylan's great admirer.

"Zapruder's film" is one of the amateur movies of the November 22, 1963 event, the most complete, shot in 8 mm by Abraham Zapruder. It had been used by the Warren Commission to establish the assassination chronology, among others. It is now preserved at the Sixth Floor Museum, a museum in honor of President Kennedy, in the building formerly known as the Texas School Book Depository. The viewing of this film is actually unpleasant, so it is unlikely the narrator has seen it 33 times, the number 33 alludes to the highest degree of Freemasonry. That said, a 2017 poll found just 33 percent of Americans believe Oswald alone killed Kennedy.

"They Killed Him" (line 84) is a song by the Highwaymen, Country supergroup gathering Kris Kristofferson, Waylon Jennings, Johnny Cash, and Willie Nelson. Dylan covered it in his album **Knocked Out Loaded**. JFK was "killed twice", first time physically on November 22, second time spiritually for his ideals still do not prevail in the United States. The narrator repeats "they killed him" four times, and warns: "Son, the age of the Anti-Christ has just only begun." Apocalyptic prophecies are a recurrent theme in Dylan songs, on his three 'religious' albums from 1979-81, and before and after them. The Anti-Christ reference should be linked to the first line from the second verse (line 22), both form a quotation from the First Epistle of Saint John (2:18): "*Little children*, it is the last time: and as ye have heard that *antichrist* shall come, even now are there many antichrists; whereby we know that it is the last time."

Air Force One is the presidential aircraft, which landed in Dallas, on Love Field airport (lines 88-90). "Let me know when you decide to throw in the towel," L.B. Johnson could have said it to JFK to take his place. Johnson insisted on swearing in on November 22 at 2:38, only two hours and eight minutes after the assassination, when on board of the aircraft. He had been defeated by JFK as choice for candidate at the Democratic nomination for the 1960 presidential election, and some theories suggest he was no stranger to the plot against the president.

The three first verses consist mostly of references to the assassination context, and a few song or film titles. In the fourth verse, the narrator requests disc-jockey Wolfman Jack to play him songs on the radio, and Dylan multiplies songs and musicians' quotations.

92	What's New, Pussycat? What'd I say?
93	I said the soul of a nation been torn away
94	It's beginning to go into a slow decay
95	And that it's thirty-six hours past Judgment Day
96	Wolfman Jack, he's speaking in tongues
97	He's going on and on at the top of his lungs
98	Play me a song, Mr. Wolfman Jack
99	Play it for me in my long Cadillac
100	Play that Only The Good Die Young
101	Take me to the place Tom Dooley was hung
102	Play St. James Infirmary in the Court of King James
103	If you want to remember, better write down the names
104	Play Etta James, too, play I'd Rather Go Blind
105	Play it for the man with the telepathic mind
106	Play John Lee Hooker, play Scratch My Back
107	Play it for that strip club owner named Jack
108	Guitar Slim Going Down Slow
109	Play it for me and for Marilyn Monroe

110	And please, Don't Let Me Be Misunderstood
111	Play it for the First Lady, she ain't feeling any good
112	Play Don Henley, play Glenn Frey
113	Take it to the Limit and let it go by
114	And play it for Carl Wilson, too
115	Looking far, far away down Gower Avenue
116	Play Tragedy, play Twilight Time
117	Take Me Back to Tulsa to the scene of the crime
118	Play another one and Another One Bites the Dust
119	Play The Old Rugged Cross and In G-d We Trust
120	Ride the Pink Horse down that Long, Lonesome Road
121	Stand there and wait for his head to explode
122	Play Mystery Train for Mr. Mystery
123	The man who fell down dead like a rootless tree
124	Play it for the Reverend, play it for the Pastor
125	Play it for the dog that got no master
126	Play Oscar Peterson, play Stan Getz
127	Play Blue Sky, play Dickey Betts
128	Play Art Pepper, Thelonious Monk
129	Charlie Parker and all that junk
130	All that junk and All That Jazz
131	Play something for The Birdman of Alcatraz
132	Play Buster Keaton, play Harold Lloyd
133	Play Bugsy Siegel, play Pretty Boy Floyd
134	Play the numbers, play the odds
135	Play Cry Me A River for the Lord of the Gods
136	Play number nine, play number six
137	Play it for Lindsey and Stevie Nicks
138	Play Nat King Cole, play Nature Boy
139	Play Down In The Boondocks for Terry Malloy
140	Play It Happened One Night and One Night of Sin
141	There's twelve million souls that are listening in
142	Play the Merchant of Venice, play the merchants of death
143	Play Stella by Starlight for Lady Macbeth
144	Don't worry, Mr. President, help's on the way
145	Your brothers are coming, there'll be hell to pay
146	Brothers? What brothers? What's this about hell?
147	Tell them, we're waiting, keep coming, we'll get them as well
148	Love Field is where his plane touched down
149	But it never did get back up off the ground
150	Was a hard act to follow, second to none
151	They killed him on the altar of the Rising Sun

152	Play Misty for me and That Old Devil Moon
153	Play Anything Goes and Memphis in June
154	Play Lonely At the Top and Lonely Are the Brave
155	Play it for Houdini spinning around his grave
156	Play Jelly Roll Morton, play Lucille
157	Play Deep In a Dream, and play Driving Wheel
158	Play Moonlight Sonata in F-sharp
159	And A Key to the Highway for the King of the Harp
160	Play Marching Through Georgia and Dumbarton's Drums
161	Play Darkness and death will come when it comes
162	Play Love Me Or Leave Me by the great Bud Powell
163	Play The Blood-stained Banner, play Murder Most Foul

The fourth and last verse begins with two well-known tracks, of two different kinds: "What's New, Pussycat?" and "What'd I say?" The former is from the 1965 film of the same name, written by Woody Allen, and composed by Burt Bacharach and Hal David, once again. The latter is a famous Ray Charles song, improvised on stage in 1958, mixing gospel and blues. "What'd I say?" was banned on many American black and white radio stations, for it broke the segregation barrier, and mixed the sacred and the profane. It was instrumental in the birth of Rock'n'Roll and impacted all the 60's English groups (Beatles, Rolling Stones, Who, Animals, ...).

The narrator follows with an idea that appears several times in the song and may be its key theme: "the soul of a nation been torn away. It's beginning to go into a slow decay." *36 Hours* is a 1965 German-American war suspense film, that tells of a plot to obtain vital information from an American military intelligence officer.

Then, from line 96 on, the narrator asks Wolfman Jack to play songs, a bit like the character on the front sleeve photograph, who is selecting a track on the jukebox. This DJ was known to talk in an incomprehensible way, like he "spoke in tongues." In Pentecostal religion it is a manifestation of the Holy Spirit, and in Spiritism the manifestation of spirits. This phenomenon might refer to Mozart, who wrote heavenly music, and was supposedly murdered.

Line 99, the "long Cadillac" may refer to Hank Williams' story, as told by David Allen Coe. In his song "The Ride," he is picked up by a mysterious man who drives through Nashville unto Alabama in a Cadillac, the car in which thirty-year-old Hank Williams was found dead. It also refers to the second verse of Warren Smith's 1958 song "Uranium Rock": "Well, I can see me now in my long Cadillac." Dylan often covered this song live with Tom Petty in 1986.

"Only the Good Die Young" is a 1977 Billy Joel song, a suitable epitaph for JFK. Dylan already used this line in "Foot of Pride," from his 1983 album *Infidels*. The same line may be found in "Abraham, Martin and John," a song written in tribute to the leading figures murdered in the 1960s: Abraham Lincoln, Martin Luther King, and John and Robert Kennedy. It was first sung in 1968 by Dion, and Dylan likes him, as he demonstrated by writing notes for his 2020 album, *Blues with Friends*. Dylan covered "Abraham, Martin and John" in a magnificent way in 1980, duetting with Clydie King. This was recently released in DVD at the *Bootleg Series Vol.13* publication, about his Gospel years.

The song "Tom Dooley" was recorded by the Kingston Trio in November 1958. It is a traditional North Carolina folk song based on the 1866 murder of a woman, Laura, by a Confederate veteran, who was convicted while he was claimed innocent, the real murderer being Tom's other lover, Laura's cousin. The Kingston Trio played folk music with sanitized arrangements, and the early Dylan made sure to distinguish himself from them.

Line 102, "St. James Infirmary" has been made famous by Louis Armstrong in 1928. It is sometimes said to be based on an eighteenth-century traditional folk song called "The Unfortunate Rake" about a soldier who spends his money on prostitutes and then dies of venereal disease – here we go again (line 75)! All kinds of musicians covered it, Dylan used its melody for his song "Blind Willie McTell," recorded in 1983 during the **Infidels** session, but released only in 1991 in *The Bootleg Series Volumes 1-3 (Rare & Unreleased) 1961-1991*, as he "never got around to completing it." It has been hailed as his best song since "Tangled Up in Blue," and was a concert staple for the Band throughout the 1990s, which finally persuaded Dylan to play it live. A series of plaintive verses depict allegorical scenes which reflect on the history of American music and slavery.

The "Court of King James" echoes evidently the song above, but this term, James or Jack, is prone to many interpretations. In history, James I King of England and Scotland, formerly James VI King of Scotland, was contemporaneous with William Shakespeare, and sponsored the translation of the Bible into English later named after him, the Authorized King James Version. It is Bob Dylan's favorite version, and he used it frequently. King Jack was also a nickname for JFK, most appropriate as he was linked to many showbiz figures, and his circle of relations was akin to a court, with its favorites and ones fallen from grace. After his assassination, JFK's widow said his husband's favorite musical was *Camelot*. Named after King Arthur's castle, it tells Arthur's fictionalized story. JFK often listened to its last lines:

Don't let it be forgot
That once there was a spot
For one brief, shining moment
That was known as Camelot

Thus, *Camelot* became associated with the President Kennedy tenure.

Lastly, as referred in line 107, Jack is Lee Oswald's murderer's first name. Jack Ruby, owner of a striptease club in Dallas, killed Oswald, live on television, two days after JFK's assassination. In September 1964, the Warren Commission concluded that Ruby acted alone in killing Oswald, shooting him on impulse, and out of grief over Kennedy's assassination. These findings were challenged by various critics who suggest that Ruby was involved with major figures in organized crime and that he was acting as part of an overall plot surrounding the assassination of Kennedy. He died in January 1967, his trial still pending.

Line 104, "I'd Rather Go Blind" was sung by Etta James in 1967 and became a blues and soul music standard. Bob Dylan sang half-a-dozen tracks with Etta James in July 1986, at the Marriott hotel in Providence, Rhode Island.

"The man with the telepathic mind" could be Criswell, who predicted in March 1963 that JFK would not run for the next presidential election, because something would happen to him in November. It could be Oswald as well, as told by writer Don DeLillo in his novel *Libra*. For DeLillo, the Kennedy assassination was a turning point in American history that shattered the country's sense of a common reality and purpose in the postwar era, an argument close to Dylan's.

John Lee Hooker is a well-known blues musician Dylan opened for in April 1961, at Gerde's Folk City in New York. In 1967 Dylan covered Hooker's song *Tupelo Blues*, a talking blues about the 1936 flood in Tupelo, Mississippi. The prophetic theme of the flood has often been covered by Bob Dylan, lately in his 2000 songs "High Water" and "The Levee's Gonna Break."

"Baby Scratch My Back" is a Slim Harpo song, released in 1965, his most successful hit. John Lee Hooker's song "Boom Boom" has a similar riff.

Line 108, "Going Down Slow" is a meaningful title by blues guitarist Guitar Slim, besides it sings:

Tell her don't see no doctor
Because the doctor can't do me no good

The narrator asks this song for Marilyn Monroe, who sang for the president's birthday in May 1962. Known to be his lover, she had an illness doctors found difficult to heal. Guitar Slim broke ground for Rock'n'Roll by using distortion ten years before Jimi Hendrix.

"Don't Let Me Be Misunderstood" was written in 1964 for Nina Simone, and covered by many artists, including the Animals. "Please don't let me be misunderstood" is what the First Lady, Jacqueline Kennedy, must have been thinking on several occasions.

Lines 112 and 113, the narrator names two founding members of the pop-rock American group The Eagles, who each undertook a solo career after the group was disbanded. "Take It to the Limit" was released in 1975 on the Eagles' fourth album. In an interview for his album release, Dylan tells of his admiration for a few Eagles tracks: "New Kid in Town," "Life in the Fast Lane," and "Pretty Maids All in a Row."

Carl Wilson founded the Beach Boys, with his two brothers Brian and Dennis. The narrator mentions him (line 114) for he sang on a Warren Zevon track, "Desperados Under the Eaves." In this track, Zevon talks of Gower Avenue, quoted in line 115. The real name is Gower Street, where the very first Hollywood cinema studio set up. Dylan likes Zevon a lot, he covered several of his songs in his 2002 tour, as a tribute to Zevon who suffered from a fatal illness. "Desperados Under the Eaves" includes the line "But except in dreams you're never really free," which reminds us of "only dead men are free" from the previous verse.

"Tragedy" is a song released in 1959 by Thomas Wayne and The DeLons, and covered in 1961 by The Fleetwoods. Bobby Zimmerman listened to this kind of pop and doo-wop on the radio, before he discovered Folk music.

"Twilight Time" is a track sung by the black vocal group The Platters, well-known in the 1950s and 1960s, and of course it is the time before dark.

"Take Me Back to Tulsa" is a Western swing standard song, sang by violinist Bob Wills in 1940. The "scene of the crime" may refer to the 1921 race massacre in Tulsa, one of the worst outbursts of racial violence in all American history. The TV series *Watchmen* features this event. The original creators of the *Watchmen*, Alan Moore and Dave Gibbons, quoted two Dylan songs in their graphic novel: "Desolation Row" and "All Along the Watchtower." It may call to mind the title song from his 2012 album as well, "Tempest," where Dylan calls out to the "watchman."

"Another One Bites the Dust" is a well-known song from the English group Queen, released in 1980. Coming from Bob Dylan, this choice of song is unlikely, but he is renowned for having eclectic tastes, and for acknowledging other musicians' popularity even though they are not to his liking.

"The Old Rugged Cross" is an old evangelic hymn, covered in 1991 by the soul singer Al Green. Dylan had a recording session with Al Green's group in 1985, but nothing came out of it.

In G-d We Trust, as you all know, is the U.S.A national motto. Here God's name is not fully written, as a Jewish commandment forbids talking God's name in vain. It is also the name of the Dead Kennedys 1981 album.

Ride the Pink Horse is a 1947 noir crime film directed by Robert Montgomery, who also stars in it, and its screenplay was based on the 1946 novel of the same title by Dorothy B. Hughes.

"The Lonesome Road" is a 1927 song, covered by Frank Sinatra, among others. Bob Dylan borrowed its melody and a few lines for his song "Sugar Baby," from his 2001 album ***"Love and Theft"***:

> Look up look up
> And seek your maker
> Before Gabriel blows his horn

Line 122, "Mystery Train" was sung by Elvis Presley in 1955 for the Sun Records label, two years after it was written by Junior Parker. It was covered by dozens of singers and is part of the mythology of Rock. Dylanologue Greil Marcus wrote a book including this title, and director Jim Jarmusch named a film from it. Dylan recorded it in 1980 for his **Shot of Love** album, and it was released recently in the *Bootleg Series Vol.16*.

Mr. Mystery is a nickname jazz musician Sun Ra liked to give himself, as it sustained mystery around him. He some-times introduced himself this way: "Some people call me Mis-ter Ra, some people call me Mister Ree. But you can call me Mister Mystery." His records were produced by Tom Wilson, Bob Dylan's second producer after John Hammond. Dylan listened to jazz and is likely to have seen Sun Ra in concert. On the other hand, Joni Mitchell, who has often been compared to Dylan though she is a bit younger, composed in 1976 a song addressing him, "Talk to Me." In that song she calls him *Mr. Mystery*, for when she was part of the *Rolling Thunder Revue,* she did not manage to talk to him deeply and pierce his mys-tery.

Line 124, the "Reverend" points to Gary Davis, a blind bluesman Dylan met in 1961. He covered several of his songs, particularly "Cocaine" and "Candy Man." As Dylan told Gary Hill in October 1993: "These people who originated this music, they're all Shakespeares, you know they're Thomas Edisons, Louis Pasteurs. they invented this type of thing. In a hundred years, they'll be notable for that. The people who played that music were still around then, and so there was a bunch of us, me included, who got to see all these people close up – people like Son House, Reverend Gary Davis or Sleepy John Estes. Just to sit there and be up close and watch them play, you could study what they were doing, plus a bit of their lives rubbed off on you. Those vibes will carry into you forever, really, so it's like those people, they're still here to me. They're not ghosts of the past or anything, they're continually here."

The "dog that got no master" refers to the HMV (His Master's Voice) RCA Victor's logo and advertising slogan. It shows a dog giving an ear to a gramophone's horn, a picture drawn in 1925 by Francis Barraud. That said, a dog without a master can be a derogatory name, for a lost soul who has neither Reverend nor Pastor.

Oscar Peterson and Stan Getz are renowned jazz pianist and saxophonist. Art Pepper, Thelonious Monk and Charlie Parker are other great jazzmen. Bob Dylan saw Thelonious Monk in a small New York club in the early 1960s, maybe their mutual friend Allen Ginsberg introduced them. In *Chronicles*, Dylan told him that he "played folk music up the street. 'We all play folk music,' he said."

"Blue Skies" is a song by Frank Sinatra, JFK's favorite. Dickey Betts, who played the guitar in the blues-rock group The Allman Brothers, wrote the song "Blue Sky" in 1972. He and Bob Dylan played together live in 1995, and Betts was surprised Dylan knew by heart his song "Ramblin' Man."

Lines 129-130, *junk* here refers to drugs, specifically heroin, as Charlie Parker and numerous jazzmen were addicted to it. This term may also refer to the trash, that is rumors and articles about JFK in the tabloids before and after his death.

All That Jazz is a song from the 1975 musical *Chicago*, a hit by Liza Minelli. Before that, it had been a way of saying things of the same kind, without naming them.

The Birdman of Alcatraz is a 1962 film. Its main character was sentenced to solitary confinement after having killed a prison guard, and took up studying birds, then was allowed to keep birds in jail. It is the fictionalized story of Robert Stroud, who died one day before President Kennedy. Jazz musicians' names, combined with the Alcatraz name, may bring to mind the renowned Clint Eastwood, who is a jazz fan. He directed a film about Charlie Parker (*Bird*), and starred in *Escape from Alcatraz*, a 1979 Don Siegel film.

Buster Keaton and Harold Lloyd were American comedians in the early twentieth century, among the first on the cinema screens. They were both physical comedians who performed death-defying stunts in their films, maybe that is why Dylan included their names in the song.

Bugsy Siegel was an American mobster who was a driving force behind the development of the Las Vegas Strip. He was not only influential within the Jewish Mob, but along with his childhood friend and fellow gangster Meyer Lansky, also held significant influence within the Italian-American Mafia and the largely Italian-Jewish National Crime Syndicate. Described as handsome and charismatic, he became one of the first front-page celebrity gangsters. Meyer Lansky was rumored to have taken part in a plot to kill JFK.

Pretty Boy Floyd was a bank robber, who got killed by FBI agents, aged 30. A Woody Guthrie song describes him as a kind of Robin Hood. It was sung by Dylan in a tribute record to Guthrie and Leadbelly, *A Vision Shared*, released in 1988 on the *Folkways* label. This song includes the lines "Some will rob you with a six-gun/ And some with a fountain pen," that Dylan borrowed for his 1962 "Talkin' New York."

Line 135, "Cry Me a River" was sung by Julie London in 1955, and used in the film *The Girl Can't Help It*, the first cinema film to evoke Rock'n'Roll. This version was also included in the 2006 film *V for Vendetta*. On the other hand, *V for Vendetta* is a graphic novel written by Alan Moore, who later wrote *Watchmen*, cf. line 117.

The "Lord of the Gods" can be found in several places in the Bible (Deuteronomy 10:17, Revelation 19:16, Psalms 136:3, Joshua 22:22, …), and also in other religions: Buddhism, Ancient Egyptian religion, and a few polytheisms.

"Number Nine" refers to the Beatles' song "Revolution 9" on the *White Album*. But "Number Six" is less obvious, it may allude to the Jimi Hendrix song "If Six Was Nine," or to the sixth floor where the murder weapon was found, or else to the TV series *The Prisoner*, where the hero was called Number 6, or even to the Number of the beast in the Book of Revelation, six three times.

There's another theory: the Beatles piece "Revolution 9" is concrete music, while in his song "I'm a Rocker," Chuck Berry sings:

> We were out on the floor
> when they played number six
> I was stone getting firm like a *cement* mix

The term *concrete* is a word play between the material made of *cement*, like in the Chuck Berry song, and the *concrete* music, that is Number 9, like in the Beatles song. I reckon it is a bit stretched but Bob Dylan likes to play jokes like that.

Lindsey Buckingham and Stevie Nicks lived, composed and sang together in the early 1970s, then joined the English group Fleetwood Mac. In 1976 they did back vocals on Warren Zevon's second album. Yet Zevon loved Jimi Hendrix, which leads us to the Hendrix song evoked in the previous line. Dylan writes by associations, but they are indirect, you have to look behind the words he wrote to find links inside his texts. This technique is similar to an 'Easter egg,' that is a message, image, or feature hidden in software, a video game, a film, or another medium.

"Nature Boy" is a song by Eden Ahbez, popularized by Nat King Cole in 1948, covered then by Frank Sinatra, among others. It is a pop and jazz standard, part of the *Great American Songbook*, from which Dylan drew for his three cover albums from 2015 to 2017. In a 2017 interview, Dylan was asked what he thought of seeing himself playing 40-50 years ago, so he quoted this song, saying: "That's a different person than who I am now." Tony Bennett sang it solo in 1962, and again with Lady Gaga in 2014, for their collaborative album, *Cheek to Cheek*. For Tony Bennett's ninetieth birthday, Dylan covered one of his greatest hits, "Once Upon a Time."

"Down in the Boondocks" was written by Joe South, who played bass guitar on Bob Dylan's album **Blonde on Blonde**. It was sung in 1965 by Billy Joe Royal.

Terry Malloy is a character in the 1954 crime drama film *On the Waterfront*, directed by Elia Kazan. He was played by Marlon Brando, as a docker fighting against corruption.

It Happened One Night is a 1934 film directed by Frank Capra. Its story tells of a romantic affair between a millionaire and a journalist, and it was the first film that got five Oscars.

"One Night of Sin" was sung by Elvis Presley in 1957. The year before, it had been recorded with coarser lyrics for the time, by a Rythm'n'Blues singer, Smiley Lewis.

Line 141, "twelve million souls" is from a dialogue in the 2012 Batman film *The Dark Knight Rises*, but it is more likely to be a quotation from Booker T. Washington, Afro-American community's leader at the turn of the nineteenth century. He said "at the close of this century" there will be "twelve million [black] souls" in the U.S., and that they no longer will "submit to oppression, political disfranchisement and taxation without representation." This number, twelve million, was quoted many times when speaking of American black people: particularly by Alice Dunbar Nelson (*Une Femme Dit*, *From a Woman's Point of View*, in the Pittsburgh Courier in 1926), the first American black poet, journalist and writer, and by Richard Wright in his book *12 Million Black Voices: A Folk History of the Negro in the United States*.

The "Merchant of Venice" refers to the Shakespeare play, and the "merchants of death" remind us of one of Dylan's first songs, "Masters of War," in which he criticized the ones "that build the big bombs."

"Stella By Starlight" is a jazz standard written in 1944 for the horror film *The Uninvited*. It was recorded by Frank Sinatra, Charlie Parker, and many others. It was covered by Ray Charles in Martin Scorsese's film *Casino*. Ironically, Dylan dedicates it to Lady Macbeth, who asks the spirits to eliminate her womanhood.

"Help on the Way" has been played by The Grateful Dead, written by their favorite composer, Robert Hunter. He worked with Dylan several times, particularly on the ***Together Through Life*** album. In early December 2019, Kamala Harris responded "Don't worry, Mr. President. I'll see you at your trial" to President Trump's derisive Tweet over her departure from the presidential race.

Lines 145-147 refer to JFK's brothers who died before or after him: Joseph Jr., who died in action during the second World War, Robert, murdered in 1968, and Edward, who, following the Chappaquiddick incident that killed his younger secretary, undermined his chances of ever becoming president. According to some theories, John and Bob's murders, and even Ted's accident, were linked together and came from the same persons or organizations.

Then the narrator writes about the presidential aircraft, that landed on Dallas airport, *Love Field*, named after a hero from the aviation beginnings, Moss L. Love, but one cannot help taking this term in its literal sense.

Line 150, "Was a hard act to follow, second to none" can be taken as a commentary on the great skill deployed for the president's assassination, or else on the greatness of the presidential wielding.

Rising Sun is a 1993 crime thriller film, based on Michael Crichton's novel. It is also a 1960 Fats Domino song, and "Rising Sun Blues" is a track written by Doc Watson. Doc Watson and Clarence Ashley influenced greatly the Folk music revival movement in the early 1960s. Dylan knew their records and covered several of their songs. They played at the 1963 Newport Festival, where he was invited. The altar of the Rising Sun is a Chinese temple, one out of nine imperial sacrificial altars in ancient Beijing.

"The House of the Rising Sun," sometimes called "Rising Sun Blues," is a traditional song Dylan recorded for his debut album. Its arrangement was based on Dave Van Ronk's without asking him, which provoked a falling-out between Dylan and Van Ronk. The Animals' electric version of this song made a great impression on Dylan. The city of New Orleans, where the House of The Rising Sun is located, played an important role in the conspiracy theories around the assassination: Oswald was from New Orleans, and so was Clay Shaw, who was the only person ever tried in court for this case.

"Misty" was recorded in 1955 by Erroll Garner. It became a jazz standard, covered by Frank Sinatra, you guessed it. Clint Eastwood's 1971 film *Play Misty for Me* was inspired by this song. In the film, Evelyn Draper quotes "Annabel Lee" by Edgar Allan Poe. Dylan always liked Poe, who inspired him for several songs, more on that later.

"That Old Devil Moon" was written in 1947 for the film *Finian's Rainbow*, and sung by Peggy Lee, Sinatra, and so on.

"Anything Goes" is a Cole Porter piece, written in 1934 for his musical of the same name, and Sinatra covered the song in 1956. The musical starred Ethel Merman, whose real name was Zimmermann, she changed it for she could not imagine such a name in shining letters on a billboard.

"Memphis In June" was composed by Hoagy Carmichael for its music, and Paul Webster for its lyrics, for the film noir *Johnny Angel*. Carmichael was an excellent singer, who wrote hundreds of songs, among others: "The Nearness of You," "Georgia on My Mind," and "Stardust," that the former Beatle George Harrison was quite fond of. He was an actor too, who just made his debut in Howard Hawks' film *To Have and Have Not*. The song was quoted by Dylan in his 1985 song,

"Tight Connection to My Heart": "There's just a hot-blooded singer singing *Memphis in June*."

"Lonely at the Top" was written by Randy Newman, with Frank Sinatra in mind. Sinatra was not so pleased and never recorded it, so Newman sang it on his 1972 album, *Sail Away*.

Lonely Are the Brave is a 1962 tragic Western starring Kirk Douglas. President Kennedy chose to watch this movie in the White House in November 1962, although all had unanimously voted against this "brutal, sadistic little Western."

In his time, the early twentieth century, Harry Houdini was the world's greatest magician. He was known for all sorts of escapes, even under water or buried alive. He was keen on debunking so-called psychics and mediums. He agreed with his wife that after his death he would communicate from beyond with a code, in order to be sure it was no swindle. Some say his death was provoked by spiritualists whose frauds he revealed.

Jelly Roll Morton was a pianist, singer and composer, who introduced himself as the inventor of jazz. "Lucille" was written in 1957 by Albert Collins and Richard Penniman, aka Little Richard, whom Bobby Z. wished to play with when he was a teenager. The line "Play Jelly Roll Morton, play Lucille" may also refer to the blues singer Lucille, who played with Jelly Roll Morton in Chicago. Lastly, Clyde McPhatter and his group The Drifters played in 1954 a song of the same name. Dylan always liked Clyde McPhatter. He covered some of his songs ("Money Honey," "Treasure of Love"), and his song "Seven Days" was based on McPhatter's.

"Deep In a Dream" was written in 1938 by Bob Crosby, and sung by Chet Baker, and Sinatra too.

"Driving Wheel" is a blues standard, written and played by Roosevelt Sykes in 1936, and covered by Junior Parker, B. B. King, and others.

The *Moonlight Sonata* is a well-known Ludwig Van Beethoven piece. Its real name is the *Piano Sonata No. 14 in C-sharp minor*. Why did Dylan write "F-sharp" instead? It might refer to the twentieth century American composer Irving Berlin, who could not read music or play the piano in any key other than F-Sharp major.

"Key to the Highway" is a track first played by the blues pianist Charles Segar in 1940, then Big Bill Broonzy covered it, and Dylan, in his 2015 *MusiCares* speech, recognized having learned it from him. But it was popularized in 1958 by Little Walter, "the King of Harp," in the Chicago electric blues style. Afterwards, Eric Clapton played it regularly in his shows. Little Walter was also known to push his amplifiers beyond their intended technical limitations, and to be the first musician of any kind to purposely use electronic distortion.

"Marching Through Georgia" is a Civil War song that tells of marching through Georgian territory, freeing slaves, meeting Southern Unionist men glad to once again see the U.S. flag, and punishing the Confederacy for their starting the war. It refers to General Sherman and was played at nearly all his public appearances, and even at his death. It was played too at campaign meetings for the 1896 presidential election of William McKinley (see below "Key West (Philosopher Pirate)").

"Dumbarton's Drums" is a traditional Scottish song. The famous Scottish poet Robert Burns was made freeman of Dumbarton. He inspired Dylan for his song "Highlands," released on his *Time Out of Mind* album. As part of an advertising campaign for HMV in 2008, Dylan was asked to name the lyric or verse that had the greatest impact on his life, and he selected Burns' poem *My Love Is Like a Red Red Rose*:

> O my Luve is like the melody
> That's sweetly played in tune
> So fair art thou, my bonnie lass
> o deep in luve am I
> And I will luve thee still, my dear
> Till a' the seas gang dry

"Darkness, Darkness" is a 1969 song by the Youngbloods, and "Darkness" is a 2020 track by rapper Eminem. It is as well "Sounds of Silence" first line, as sung by Simon & Garfunkel: "Hello *darkness*, my old friend." Paul Simon's career started around the same time as Dylan's, and they both toured together in 1999, switching first and second part of the show. Maybe this term is a posthumous tribute to Leonard Cohen, since a song from Cohen's next -to-last album *Old Ideas* is titled "The Darkness." Lastly, "Darkness" is a poem written by Lord Byron in July 1816 on the theme of an apocalyptic end of the world, which fits the general mood of "Murder Most Foul."

"Death will come when it comes" is said by Julius Caesar in the Shakespeare play of the same name:

> Of all the wonders that I yet have heard
> It seems to me most strange that men should fear
> Seeing that death, a necessary end

Will come when it will come

Julius Caesar's assassination comes to mind, executed in broad daylight and in a most foul way, and foreshadowing the decline of the Roman Republic.

"Love Me or Leave Me" is a 1928 jazz tune, written for a Broadway musical. Bud Powell, the jazz pianist, never recorded it, but he borrowed its chord progression, and modified its melody, that made it a new piece named "Get It"; musicians call it a *contrafact*.

The Blood-Stained Banner was one of the Confederate flags. "Holding Up the Blood-Stained Banner" could mean waving this Confederate banner, yet it may refer to a gospel song that defends the banner of faith.

At the end of the song, the narrator asks to play "Murder Most Foul," which is a self-reference by Bob Dylan.

What can we make of this building up of references? Several themes stand out:

- Machinations and criminal stories;
- Racial prejudices and racism, and the foundation of the U. S. A. on slavery;
- The Civil War, whose central cause was the dispute over whether slavery would be permitted to expand into the western territories, leading to more slave states, or

be prevented from doing so, which would set slavery on the course to ultimate extinction. This theme is included in the previous one;

- The end of an era, more specifically the end of the total trust of the American people in their leaders.

Bob Dylan catches on President Kennedy's assassination, but he goes back a hundred years, and revisits themes he already evoked in his works. Thanks to *Chronicles* and to his albums from the year 2001 on, we know he has been interested in the American Civil War since his youth. One of his recent songs, "'Cross the Green Mountain," was written for the film *Gods and Generals* that follows the story of Confederate commander Stonewall Jackson from the beginning of the Civil War to his death at the Battle of Chancellorsville. Dylan considers racism to be the original American sin. He mentioned it numerous times in interviews and songs, and made clear that, as long as it endures, this country will not know peace. The theme that ideas of adventure and freedom that were at the country's foundation and the pioneer spirit has now vanished, recurs in Dylan's work. The machination theme is obviously linked to the conspiracy theories and the general deleterious mood that prevailed around JFK.

But did the death of President John F. Kennedy really affect Bob Dylan? As it is often the case when one tries to know his feelings, the answer is not that simple.

Two days after the assassination, that is the same day as the killing of Oswald by Ruby, Dylan had a concert in up-state New York, and he had a hard time dealing with it: "I had to go on stage, I couldn't cancel. I went to the hall and to my amazement the hall was filled. Everybody turned out for the concert. The song I was opening with was 'The Times They Are A-Changin'' and I thought, 'Wow, how can I open with that song? I'll get rocks thrown at me.' That song was just too much for the day after the assassination. But I had to sing it. My whole concert takes off from there. I know I had no under-standing of anything. Something had just gone haywire in the country and they were applauding that song. And I couldn't understand why they were clapping or why I wrote that song, even. I couldn't understand anything. For me, it was just in-sane."

According to his first biographer Anthony Scaduto, when he went back to New York, "Dylan, Suze [Rotolo, Dylan's girlfriend at the time] and [her sister] Carla sat and watched the national tragedy through the rest of the weekend and into the Monday morning funeral. Through it all Dylan sat and watched and said little, just feeling the emotion of it. He drank a little wine, and played Berlioz's Requiem over and over." Dylan: "I didn't feel it any more than anybody else. We were all sensitive to it. The assassination took more of the shape of a happening. I read about those things happening to Lincoln, to Garfield, and that it could happen in this day and age was not too far-fetched. It didn't knock the wind out of me. Of course, I felt as rotten as everyone else. But if I was more sen-sitive about it than anyone else, I would have written a song about it, wouldn't I? The whole thing about my reactions to the assassination is overplayed."

Yet Scaduto countered that, despite Dylan's denial, "the murder did have an enormous effect on him. He signaled that feeling to very close friends, and a couple of weeks after Kennedy's death, Dylan gave a disastrous speech that indicated how much the assassination had troubled him. He went to the grand ballroom of the Hotel Americana in New York to accept the Tom Paine Award of the Emergency Civil Liberties Committee for his work in the civil rights campaign."

Dylan: "As soon as I got there, I felt uptight. I began to drink. I looked down from the platform and saw a bunch of people who had nothing to do with my kind of politics. I looked down and I got scared. They were supposed to be on my side, but I didn't feel any connection with them. Here were these people who'd been all involved with the left in the thirties, and now they were supporting civil-rights drives. That's groovy, but they also had minks and jewels, and it was like they were giving the money out of guilt. I got up to leave, and they followed me and caught me. They told me I had to accept the award. When I got up to make my speech, I couldn't say anything by that time but what was passing through my mind."

Here is Dylan's speech (excerpts): "So, I accept this reward – not reward, (laughter) award in behalf of Phillip Luce who led the group to Cuba which all people should go down to Cuba. I don't see why anybody can't go to Cuba. I don't see what's going to hurt by going any place. I don't know what's going to hurt anybody's eyes to see anything. On the other hand, Phillip is a friend of mine who went to Cuba. I'll stand up and to get uncompromisable about it, which I have to be to be honest, I just got to be, as I got to admit that the man who shot President Kennedy, Lee Oswald, I don't know exactly where – what he thought he was doing, but I got to admit honestly that I too – I saw some of myself in him. I don't think it would have gone – I don't think it could go that far. But I got to stand up and say I saw things that he felt, in me – not to go that far and shoot. (b oos and hisses) You can boo but booing's got nothing to do with it. It's a – I just a – I've got to tell you, man, it's Bill of Rights is free speech and I just want to admit that I accept this Tom Paine Award in behalf of James Forman of the Students Non-Violent Coordinating Committee and on behalf of the people who went to Cuba."

This speech was received very badly and Dylan had to write a letter of excuse to the ECLC. Yet it was based on real facts: Suze Rotolo had introduced Dylan to friends from the SNCC, and some among them formed a group to support the Cuban revolution. Dylan was impressed by these people who had altruist ideals, and who defied the Cuban frontier crossing interdiction. Oswald sympathized with this group's ideas, a pamphlet these people gave out was found among his posses-sions. Suze and Dylan were friends with one of these activists, Steve Kenin, who ran a music store in Greenwich Village. In 1963 Steve Kenin took off on his motorcycle to ride around Mexico and wrote an article about his adventures for Motor-cycle Magazine, and reportedly met Lee Harvey Oswald in Mexico City. According to a Mexican lawyer who was there, he last saw Kenin ride off on his motorcycle with Lee Oswald on the back, heading for the Cuban embassy to try to get visas to Cuba. The way these young people supported the Cuban revo-lution evokes in some way Tom Paine, who in his time backed the French revolution, and was reviled for his opinions. So Dylan's speech was not off-topic.

Bobby Zimmerman's mother, Beatty, was present in October 1960 when future President Kennedy visited his region, Dylan tells us in his *Chronicles*: "John Kennedy, before he became president, when he was still a senator, had come up to Hibbing on the campaign trail but that was about six months after I left. My mother said that eighteen thousand people had turned out to see him at the Veterans Memorial Building and that people were hanging from the rafters and others were in the street, that Kennedy was a ray of light and had understood completely the area of the country he was in. He gave a heroic speech, my mom said, and brought people a lot of hope. The Iron Range was an area that very few nationally known politicians or any famous people ever made it through. If I had been a voting man, I would have voted for Kennedy just for coming there. I wished I could have seen him."

Not long after the assassination, Dylan wrote a short poem:

> The colors of Friday were dull
> as cathedral bells were gently burnin'
> strikin' for the gentle
> strikin' for the kind
> strikin' for the crippled ones
> an strikin' for the blind

The Friday in this poem is undoubtedly November 22, 1963. This poem foreshadowed what would become the song "Chimes of Freedom," recorded in June 1964 for the ***Another Side of Bob Dylan*** album. The bells and the cathedral from its second line are scattered in several lines in the final song, and the third and fourth lines are found word for word. Another word whose meaning is close to *strike, toll*, appears eleven times in the song. The only other word that appears as many times is *flash*, which resounded particularly in relation to that Friday event. This word evokes the flashes of gunshots, flashes of photographs, news flashes on the television and radio, and the speed with which the American nation was overwhelmed by this event, in a flash.

In his book *Tarantula*, written around 1964-65, Dylan alludes to the Warren commission report: "that warren report, you know as well as me, just didn't make it. you know. like they might as well have asked some banana salesman from des moines, who was up in toronto on the big day, if he saw anyone around looking suspicious/ or better yet, they just coulda come & asked me what i saw/ the doctors say i gotta tumor coming up tho, so i got more important things to do than to be bothered with straightening out this whole mess." This text should not be taken too seriously, but it shows clearly Dylan still was interested in JFK's assassination, and had strong doubts about its elucidation by the official authorities.

In 2012, Dylan did an exhibition in the Gagosian gallery in New York, entitled *Revisionist Art*, in which he showed an apocryphal front cover of Life magazine, with a photograph of Lee Oswald holding the gun that killed JFK, and with this commentary: "*The Secret Life of Outlaw Assassin Lee Oswald.*"

So, what can we conclude from those facts? Dylan had a deep feeling for JFK, even though he was under no illusion and never committed for any politician. Dylan was, as he was often, more attracted by JFK's personality, by the sensation and hope he aroused, than by his political action. JFK can be viewed as the first president of the "pop" culture: he was young, good-looking, smiling, TV savvy, seemingly in his prime, even though we now know he was ill. It could not be seen, and that did matter. The list of songs and films included in "Murder Most Foul" is a part of this culture. But this song's topic is not only President Kennedy and his assassination, it is what this event means, beyond bare facts, for the state of mind of the American nation.

"Murder Most Foul" summarizes the history of the United States through their musical and cinematographic culture and brings out the loss of the spirit which was, for Bob Dylan, at this country's foundation, a spirit of adventure and hope. President Kennedy's assassination is the event which started an era of chaos, that deepened gradually in the years that followed. As early as the 1960s, Dylan shared with us his dissatisfaction and his fears: "Hard Rain's A-Gonna Fall" warned us of dark events, "Masters of War" lambasted those who bring the "Fear to bring children Into the world," "It's Alright Ma" tried and give a meaning to what happened every day on television and in our streets, "Desolation Row" tried to find an escape from the overwhelming chaos... At the turn of the 1970s and 1980s, Dylan preached Armageddon will come soon, and offered a solution for all the evils of this world. Believing in such a solution lasted about two years, but doubt soon took over. In 1983, the song "Blind Willie McTell" gave us a vision of racist prejudices that corrupted the country, together with a tribute to Blues music. Since 2000, Dylan took to more personal stories, he wrote several songs that dealt with the ideas of impairment, of failure. Songs such as "Tryin' to Get to Heaven" on the album *Time Out of Mind*, "Mississippi" on *"Love and Theft"*, and "Workingman's Blues #2" on *Mod-*

ern Times, gave us stories of lost souls, of inner exiles, of forsaken people who fight to survive in a stark economic situation, estranged from their past and their community and any steadiness. Dylan wrote these songs in a disjointed style, stuffed with quotations from other songs, of pieces of texts borrowed from books and poems, as if the present times were made of shards of meaning we had to search for groping.

With "Murder Most Foul," Dylan learns from his country's history and observes that racism, the foundation of the U.S., still exists, and that most things did not improve since the end of WWII, in spite of a short period that aroused big expectations. Sixty years after he started, Dylan continues to think there is no solution, or if ever there is one, it is beyond the human beings' reach (including his own). JFK's murder was most foul, and it opened the way to a process of slow decay, of loss of roots and of suspicion, which many of the American people have been living with ever since.

The way Dylan sings, with his minimal backing, resembles an incantation, a kind of litany of the Saints: in the Christian liturgy, "pray for us" is repeated for each of the Saints, while in his song Dylan repeats "play for us." The saints make life more bearable for the believers, as the songs help us going through our pain of living. By the way, the 2019 tour arrangements of "Girl from The North Country" are really close to "Murder Most Foul" backing music, which shows Dylan often gives us hints about what he is going to do.

Some say this track is a warning for the younger generation: look at what your elders have done, they spent their time listening to music and partying while the world was falling apart, take care not to make the same mistakes. But if

Dylan wrote "Murder Most Foul" with that in mind, wouldn't it be weird to play such an unattractive music, and for such a long time? Unless Dylan intended precisely not to distract his listeners, and repeated the Talkin' Blues formula, he used in his early years, that is playing minimal accompaniment for allowing us to focus on lyrics. I personally do not believe Dylan had such an idea in mind, for he always said a song could not change the world. He shows a state of things, without proposing any solution, a stance he already adopted in his early songs, although the media called them "protest-songs," a term he always denied. By repeating the same word in an imperative way (*play!*), the narrator in a way conjures everything he can think of to push the darkness away, as if he wanted to state that all the art, all the culture, be it classical or popular, should have a meaning, should be a necessity, against all the bloody mess surrounding us.

There are numerous songs about JFK's death, but the first one Dylan thought of must be the song written by his old friend Phil Ochs (deceased in 1976). Phil Ochs' song, "Crucifixion," is a kind of litany that laments Americans kill their idols, then delight in the images of these killings. The version available on the web, shot in front of an audience, was sung with a strong emotion and is better than the album's version. The song title alludes obviously to Jesus Christ. "Murder Most Foul" as well can be interpreted in relation to the Christ: the sacrificial lamb, 33 (Jesus Christ's age at death), the age of the Anti-Christ, stay observant (Peter 5:8), and so on. Ochs once played his song to Robert Kennedy, who broke down in tears when he understood it was about his brother.

Some say "Murder Most Foul" is Bob Dylan's "American Pie." This song was written by Don McLean in 1971 and alludes to events and people from the 1950s and 1960s up to 1970. Dylan knows it for sure, but there is no indication it influenced him when he wrote "Murder Most Foul."

"Murder Most Foul" makes us think of another Dylan song, written by Bob Dylan and Sam Shepard, "Brownsville Girl." It was released in the *Knocked Out Loaded* album, and lasts eleven minutes. Some say it is Bob Dylan's forgotten masterpiece, at any rate it is different from all the other Dylan songs, as is "Murder Most Foul." It talks as well of assassination and of the replacement of the old world by a new world.

"Murder Most Foul" lyrics may seem simple and cliché, but they are in harmony with the song topic. Their style is a mix of Beat poetry – Ginsberg, Kerouac, Ferlinghetti – and noir novels – Hammett, Chandler, Himes, J. H. Chase, Jim Thompson, David Goodis. By the end of 1963, the Beat poets' era came to an end, and the noir, or crime, novels were an established genre. This fictional genre is characterized by a violent environment, a tragic and pessimistic outlook on society, a strong referential anchor and a political or social commitment. These features make a perfect scene for the conspiracy theories born from the Kennedy assassination, and the contemporaneous plots to invade Cuba or to take the lead of the Teamsters Union.

This track's style makes us also think of the Irish writer James Joyce. In "I Feel a Change Comin' On," Dylan sings he is "reading James Joyce." This song was released in 2009 in the *Together Through Life* album and is in part based on the *Letters to Nora*, which Joyce wrote to his wife Nora in 1909. Dylan wrote about Joyce too in *Chronicles*, saying the "president of Columbia Records, had given me this as a gift, a first-edition copy of the book [*Ulysses*] and I couldn't make hide nor hair of it," and "what he say, I knew not what." Dylan visited several times the James Joyce Museum in Dublin, its curator knows him and likes him: in 2007 he offered to lend him Joyce's bicycle for a ride! Seriously speaking, Joyce's works are themselves filled with references and quotations. So much so that a parallel was made by Matt Satterfield, between Joyce's autobiographical novel *A Portrait of the Artist as a Young Man*, and Dylan's life: As Stephen Dedalus, the hero of this book, rejected Catholicism, Dylan rejected the protest-songs; he dropped the familiar things to follow his own artistic vision, then, as Stephen left Dublin for Paris, Bob withdrew from the world to write dozens of songs, that were known only a few years later under the name of the *Basement Tapes*.

Finally, the million-dollar question: does Dylan believe in the conspiracy theories which he alludes to throughout his song? We will never know for sure, and it does not matter, for these theories exist, they are part of the landscape, millions of people know them, and they contribute to the state of things in the U.S.A. This song can be interpreted ironically, it contains associations and indirect references, hidden things, Easter eggs. We can never be certain that we have found them all, nor that we did not make up some. It is part of the game, for a long time Dylan did not write any song with only one level of meaning, and this one may be the most perfect example. He likes to sustain mystery in his work and his life, sometimes to give red herrings. After all, Dylan may have written this song only for his own amusement, for seeing how many thousands of pages, be it physical or virtual, will be written about this song and this album... if it is the case, he succeeded beyond all hopes, for there were more than ever before!

3 - I Contain Multitudes

"I Contain Multitudes" is the second track released on the internet, April 27, 2020, just one month after "Murder Most Foul." Its accompanying picture was shot at the Salzburg July 9, 1996 show, by an amateur photographer, a regular at Dylan shows, Andrea Orlandi.

The melody recalls "Nettie Moore" in the **Modern Times** album. Like "Murder Most Foul," this song dwells mainly on one note, C in this case, which is unusual because Dylan tends to avoid C major, and is inclined to play the piano black keys. Those two songs have the same repetitive structures and basic melodies, the same musical, historic and political references to the pop culture, and a few bragging words and dim threats of retaliation. These features can be found in many rap songs, except for their tempo and their jazzy arrangements, that were inspired by the Great American Songbook, in which Dylan drew from 2015 on. Chris Shaw, who was part of their recording and mixing, was hired by Dylan for the **"Love and Theft"** album because he worked with the rap group Public Enemy. This is no first time for Dylan to flirt with rap: he recorded with Kurtis Blow in 1986, and played rap in his radio program, on XM radio, from 2006 to 2009.

"I Contain Multitudes" quotes from the American poet Walt Whitman:

Do I contradict myself?

Very well then, I contradict myself
(I am large, I contain multitudes)

Whitman published this as an untitled poem in 1855, and only in 1881 included it in his volume *Leaves of Grass* with the name "Song of Myself." It is his most famous work and sometimes called The Great American Poem.

As usual, Dylan shows us no shortage of quotations and references.

1	Today and tomorrow, and yesterday, too
2	The flowers are dyin' like all things do
3	Follow me close, I'm going to Bally-na-Lee
4	I'll lose my mind if you don't come with me
5	I fuss with my hair, and I fight blood feuds
6	I contain multitudes

The first line makes us think of the 1975 song "Tangled Up in Blue." In a 1978 interview in Rolling Stone magazine, Dylan said: "you've got yesterday, today and tomorrow all in the same room, and there's very little that you can't imagine not happening." Dylan often said tomorrow did not exist and that times in his lyrics had no real meaning. This is a key theme in Asian philosophies, that will be developed further on. It alludes also to a line in Shakespeare's Macbeth (Act V, scene 5):

Tomorrow, and tomorrow, and tomorrow
Creeps in this petty pace from day to day

The second line may refer to Walt Whitman's poem "When Lilacs Last in the Dooryard Bloom'd," his tribute to

Abraham Lincoln on the occasion of his assassination. Given there are two other songs on this album mentioning a presidential assassination, this may be a sly wink. More directly, it quotes the song "Danny Boy": "flowers are dyin'." This song was written in 1913 by the English composer Frederic Weatherly, aiming to reunite Irish independentists and unionists. Its lyrics were modified to go with a well-known Irish melody, "Londonderry Air," and the song became very popular in the Irish public, among others. This melody was supposedly written by a blind harpist in the sixteenth century, Rory Dall O'Cahan, nicknamed Blind Rory. "Danny Boy" was covered by Judy Garland, Johnny Cash, Elvis Presley, Eric Clapton, and many others. Johnny Cash's version was used lastly in the *Peaky Blinders* series, one more allusion to blindness. It evokes a message from an Irish staying in his country to another one, migrated or gone to war, or maybe in the Irish Liberation Army. Nowadays, it is often sung at funerals. This is precisely the case in another Dylan song where he quotes its title, "Foot of Pride," written in 1983 for the **Infidels** album, but released only in 1991 in the **Bootleg Series Vol.I**: "They sang 'Danny Boy' at his funeral."

Line 3 mentions a Northern Ireland village, Ballinalee. The spelling written by Dylan refers to the poem "The Lass from Bally-na-Lee," written in the early nineteenth century by Antoine O Rafteiri, the last of the wandering bards. He became blind after eight of his nine children died from smallpox. The poem was a favorite of Dylan's friend from the early 1960s, Liam Clancy, of The Clancy Brothers. In May 2017, Dylan spent an evening with the singer Shane McGowan, founder of the Irish rock group The Pogues, and we may guess they talked about Irish poetry. The last line in "I Contain Multitudes,"

"Keep your mouth away from me" quotes a line from another Irish poem: "Keep your Kiss to Yourself."

The beginning of "I Contain Multitudes" refers three times to blindness, may we see that as a coincidence? It is most likely a way of paying tribute to blind artists, particularly to the oldest one, Homer. In the CliffsNotes, Ulysses, hero of The Odyssey, is described as "a living series of contradictions, a much more complicated character than we would expect to find in the stereotypical epic hero."

7	Got a tell-tale heart, like Mr. Poe
8	Got skeletons in the walls of people you know
9	I'll drink to the truth and the things we said
10	I'll drink to the man that shares your bed
11	I paint landscapes, and I paint nudes
12	I contain multitudes

The second verse calls on the macabre story writer Edgar Allan Poe, but it is far from the first time for Dylan. In 1965 already, in his song "Just Like Tom Thumb's Blues," Dylan cited Poe's *The Murders in the Rue Morgue*: "When you're down on *Rue Morgue* Avenue." In a 2003 interview by Robert Hilburn, he says in the early 1960s "Poe's stuff knocked me out in more ways than I could name." In 2004, for the TV program *60 Minutes*, talking about the burden of being called a prophet: "It was like being in an Edgar Allan Poe story. And you're just not that person everybody thinks you are, though they call you that all the time." In *Chronicles*, he wrote that in 1961, he went to see the place where Poe lived in New York, Third Street. In his novel *Tarantula*, written in 1964-65, he quoted from a little-known poem, "Al Aaraaf," written by Poe in 1829. In the **Another Side of Bob Dylan** album, the song "Chimes of Freedom" was based on the poem "The Bells." The word *bells* is used three times, in a context that is not so far from Poe's poem. In his next album, the song "Love Minus Zero / No Limit" mentions a "raven," the title of one of most famous of Poe's poems. In the **Oh Mercy** album in 1989, Dylan gets back to the *bells* theme, in the song "Ring Them Bells." **Time Out of Mind** album title is drawn from Poe's story, *The Fall of the House of Usher* (although Poe took it from Shakespeare's *Romeo and Juliet*). All this is only a part of Poe's influences on Dylan, that were detailed by Christopher Rollason. He detected the common themes to Poe and Dylan, especially the dreams, and numerous uses of the literary genre which Poe among others initiated, the "Gothic fiction," an extreme form of Romantism that embodies an appreciation of the joys of extreme emotion, the thrills of fearfulness and awe inherent in the sublime, and a quest for atmosphere. Mary Shelley's novel *Frankenstein* is another example of Gothic fiction, more about it soon.

"I Contain Multitudes" refers to three of Poe's novellas: line 7, *The Tell-Tale Heart*, and line 8, "skeletons in the walls" alludes to *The Cask of Amontillado* and *The Black Cat*. Those three stories offer the same themes of guiltiness and madness. The narrator plays on a double meaning: it may be skeletons of people you know, in the walls, or else skeletons, in the walls of people you know, without them knowing, which is even more ironic.

Line 9, "I'll drink to the truth and the things that we said," echoes the line in "Murder Most Foul": "What is the truth, and where did it go?"

Line 11 may refer to the Wes Anderson film *Moonrise Kingdom*, in which the main character paints watercolors that are "mostly landscapes, but a few nudes." It may also be a self-reflection on Bob Dylan's paintings.

13	Red Cadillac and a black moustache
14	Rings on my fingers that sparkle and flash
15	Tell me, what's next? What shall we do?
16	Half my soul, baby, belongs to you
17	I rollic and I frolic with all the young dudes
18	I contain multitudes

The third verse opens with a song Dylan covered in 2001. "Red Cadillac and a Black Moustache" was sung in 1957 by Warren Smith. This version by Bob Dylan is included in a tribute compilation to the Sam Phillips label, Sun Records, which published the first Rock'n'Roll tracks.

Next line, "rings on my fingers" is a line from a 1909 song by Ada Jones, one of the first singers ever recorded. It may come from an association with *Ada* Lovelace, who was the poet Lord Byron's daughter, Byron being a forerunner of the Gothic fiction. Line 14 may also allude to two previous Dylan songs: "She Belongs to Me" – "She wears an Egyptian *ring*/ It *sparkles* before she speaks" – and "Señor (Tales of Yankee Power)" – "a gypsy with a broken flag and *flashing ring.*"

Line 16, "Half my soul belongs to you" quotes from the book *Gabriel's Palace: Jewish Mystical Tales* by Howard Schwartz, a collection of Jewish mythical tales.

"All the Young Dudes" is a song written by David Bowie for the singer Ian Hunter and his group Mott The Hoople. It is a glam rock hymn, close to another Bowie song, "Rock'n'Roll Suicide," by its dark tune, its call to an imaginary public, and its reference to suicide. Bowie explained in 1974 in Rolling Stone: "It is no hymn to the youth as people thought. It is completely the opposite." The "young dudes [who] carry the news" say there is "five years to go before the end of the earth. It has been announced that the world will end because of a lack of natural resources."

19	I'm just like Anne Frank, like Indiana Jones
20	And them British bad boys the Rolling Stones
21	I go right to the edge, I go right to the end
22	I go right where all things lost are made good again
23	I sing the songs of experience like William Blake
24	I have no apologies to make
25	Everything's flowing all at the same time
26	I live on the Boulevard of Crime
27	I drive fast cars, and I eat fast foods
28	I contain multitudes

Dylan quotes in one sentence Anne Frank, Indiana Jones, and "them British bad boys The Rolling Stones," which could appear out of place, even insulting for Anne Frank, who was killed by the Nazis. Actually, Dylan recognizes a part of his personality in each of these three characters. Anne Frank wrote in her diary she was feeling like a "bundle of contradictions." Indiana Jones has two faces: the professor buried in his books, and the archeologist eager to go on a new adventure. Anne Frank and Indiana Jones are opposites, the former represents the tragic reality of the victims of Nazism, and the latter an imaginary story for reducing them to zero. Anne Frank personifies the losses – loss of a normal life, of her family, of the innocence, of the Jews, of her life – Indiana Jones the findings – resolution of historical enigmas, findings of treasures. The Rolling Stones are anarchists who live a bourgeois rock star life. What is more their two leaders, Jagger and Richards, opposed each other for years. These three characters contain multitudes. As an aside, when Dylan opened for The Rolling Stones at the Desert Trip Festival in 2016, Jagger said they never had a Nobel Prize winner open for them before, and that Dylan was "your own Walt Whitman."

Line 23, Dylan pays tribute to one of his inspirations, William Blake, who himself contained multitudes since he was a poet, a painter and an engraver, same as Dylan is a musician, performer, writer, painter, and metal sculptor. Besides Blake was at the same time enthusiastic about the French Revolution, and very religious, even mystical – while the Revolution ended the power of the Catholic church. He was fiercely against slavery and racism, which resounds with themes found in "Murder Most Foul." He was critical of established religion, and praised Jesus, ideas which remind us of Bob Dylan's. His poem *The Tyger* was quoted in Dylan's song "Roll on John," in the 2012 album **Tempest**. The song "Every Grain of Sand," written by Dylan in 1981, is based on Blake's poem, *Auguries of Innocence*:

> To see a world in a grain of sand
> And a heaven in a wild flower
> Hold infinity in the palm of your hand
> And eternity in an hour

"Everything's flowing all at the same time" alludes to the philosopher Heraclitus, who said everything flows, meaning that everything is constantly changing, from the smallest grain of sand to the stars in the sky. Thus, every object ultimately is a figment of one's imagination. Only change itself is real, constant and eternally in flux, like the continuous flow of a river which always renews itself. The previous line expressed it: "I go right where all things lost are made good again." One may think of the changes in melody and lyrics Dylan keeps on doing when performing his songs, and as a whole of all the changes Dylan went through from the 1960s to the present time. All the same, Blake's well-known collection of poems full name was *Songs of Innocence and of Experience Shewing the Two Contrary States of the Human Soul*, meaning his view of the two states of man, the original state being childlike innocence, and an eventual loss of, or changing of that innocence into the final state of experience. Heraclitus invented the philosophy of "contraries," or the unity of opposites, that Blake, Whitman, and Dylan were all clearly inspired by.

Line 26, the song "Boulevard du Crime" was recorded by the French singer Edith Piaf in 1960. The Boulevard of Crime is a nickname for the *Boulevard du Temple* in Paris, France, remade by the baron Haussman in 1862. It was renowned for its popular theaters, in which were given plays telling criminal stories. The film *Children of Paradise* (*Les Enfants du Paradis*), a Bob Dylan favorite, took place partly in this Boulevard. Dylan was inspired by its characters on the *Rolling Thunder Revue* 1975 tour, and in the film from this tour, *Renaldo and Clara*. The narrator in lines 26-27 acknowledges he lives in a secular place, and he likes secular pleasures such as fast cars, fast-foods, and crime stories.

29	Pink pedal-pushers, red blue jeans
30	All the pretty maids, and all the old queens
31	All the old queens from all my past lives
32	I carry four pistols and two large knives
33	I'm a man of contradictions, I'm a man of many moods
24	I contain multitudes

"Pink Pedal Pushers" is a song by Carl Perkins, guitarist and composer who influenced The Beatles and many other Rock musicians. Here is what Dylan said of Carl Perkins at his death, in 1998: "He really stood for freedom. That whole sound stood for all degrees of freedom. It would just jump off the turntable… we wanted to go where that was happening." *Pedal Pushers* were women's mid-calf length pants used to ride bicycles in the late 1950s.

"Red Blue Jeans and a Ponytail" is a 1957 song by Gene Vincent, in the Rockabilly style. Both of these songs talk of young girls, which serves as a transition for next line, "All the pretty maids, and all the old queens."

The "pretty maids" is from the last line of an English nursery rhyme. It has been included in songs and films, with sexual innuendos, particularly "Walking the Dog" by Rufus Thomas, covered by The Rolling Stones in their first album. It reminds us too of the "Pretty Maids All in a Row" alluded to in "Murder Most Foul."

"Old queens" reminisces a line from Neal Cassady's autobiographical novel, *The First Third*. Neal was the hero of many of Jack Kerouac's novels; he is the Dean Moriarty of *On the Road*. In his only novel, Cassady talks of Allen Ginsberg, and the people he introduced to Neal: "*old queens*, serious poets from Ireland, County Cork, drunk poets from the local gentry..." Cassady was another person with contradictions, a multitude.

Line 32, the "four pistols and two large knives" were carried by Ward Hill Lamon, bodyguard and friend of President Abraham Lincoln, as told by Shelby Foote in his book *The Civil War: A Narrative*. Lamon was away when Lincoln was killed, which gave birth to conspiracy theories. Some compared the Lincoln assassination and Kennedy's, finding similarities between both. Dylan's interest in the Civil War is unchanged.

35	You greedy old wolf, I'll show you my heart
36	But not all of it, only the hateful part
37	I'll sell you down the river, I'll put a price on your head
38	What more can I tell you? I sleep with life and death in the same bed
39	Get lost, madame, get up off my knee
40	Keep your mouth away from me
41	I'll keep the path open, the path in my mind
42	I'll see to it that there's no love left behind
43	I'll play Beethoven's sonatas, and Chopin's preludes
44	I contain multitudes

Line 35, the "greedy old wolf" is a translation from old Norse of Geri and Freki, wolves who accompanied the god Odin. In the Scandinavian mythology, the man-god Odin was associated with wolves and ravens and they acted as a single organism: the ravens were the eyes, mind, and memory – which brings us back to Edgar Allan Poe's raven – and the wolves were the providers of meat and nourishment, while

Odin was a poet and only drank wine. Otherwise said, all of them formed a multitude.

Line 36, "the hateful part" can be found in the epic poem *Jerusalem Delivered*, written in Italian in 1581 by Torquato Tasso. Tasso's poem has elements inspired by the classical epics of Homer and Virgil, whom Dylan referenced many times in the year 2000. In this poem, a hero is named Rinaldo, that is similar to the character's name in Dylan's film, *Renaldo and Clara*. It reminds us Dylan is also a filmmaker, which adds to the multitude.

When asked what he thought about his line "I sleep with life and death in the same bed," Dylan answered (New York Times interview, June 2020): "I think about the death of the human race. The long strange trip of the naked ape. Not to be light on it, but everybody's life is so transient. Every human being, no matter how strong or mighty, is frail when it comes to death. I think about it in general terms, not in a personal way."

Line 39, "Get lost, Madame" is the English translation of a sentence from the short story *Rue Pigalle*, by the French writer Francis Carco. This author lived in Paris in the early twentieth century and painted the street-life, the "Man on the Street" (Dylan's 1961 song). From the beginning, Dylan was interested in the outcast people, he sang about them in several songs, "Chimes of Freedom" especially.

Then Dylan reasserts he keeps the path open in his mind, same as Whitman before him. The song ends by mentioning Beethoven again, and Chopin.

Oddly enough, in the film *Rolling Thunder Revue: A Bob Dylan Story*, released on Netflix in June 2019, Dylan talks of Ginsberg – who himself greatly admired Whitman – and mentions Whitman and "I Contain Multitudes." Was this song already written, or did the film gave Dylan the starting idea to write it? Whatever, this song's message is clear: The narrator went through a multitude of experiences, thought about multitudes of ideas and opinions, and is not immune to contradictions. Even though the public admires his work, he is just another human being, at times uncertain of his talents and of his public role. He asks for indulgence from his public and critics, who ought to ponder about his situation before giving any judgement regarding him. But is the narrator only Bob Dylan? As Jochen Markhorst – who wrote numerous books about Bob Dylan – reminds us, for a long time Dylan made his own Rimbaud's famous words "Je est un autre," "I is another," when he sings '*I*' in his songs, he does not mean 'himself,' Bob Dylan. As quoted above, he may think of "every human being," "in general terms, not in a personal way."

4 - False Prophet

"False Prophet" is the third and last track on the internet, released on May 8, 2020, which is new for Bob Dylan: he already released a single track online, but never three for the same album. The date for the album **Rough and Rowdy Ways** release, June 19, was announced that same day. The picture coming with the song draws from the cover of a pulp fiction magazine, *The Shadow* dated July 15, 1942. The title's font was kept from the original picture. But the picture was reversed, the character looks on the left, and what he holds in his hand was replaced by a syringe, moreover the shadow was modified to represent a hanged man. This background was taken from another pulp fiction magazine, *Black Mask*, dated May 1943, and slightly modified. This magazine published noir crime stories, so we stay in the same mood as "Murder Most Foul."

So far, no information leaked about the selection and modification of these pictures, so we can imagine anything. It may be an association with *Shadow and Act* by Ralph Ellison, as that writer is referenced in "Murder Most Foul." Dylan likes pulp fiction magazine covers, he already used one for the album **Knocked Out Loaded** sleeve, in 1986. In *Chronicles*, Dylan mentions twice *The Shadow*, that he read in comic strips. Excerpts from The Shadow stories are cited in the song "Dreamin' of You" and on the album **Together Through Life**. The Shadow was the first super-hero, the archetype of Batman.

The American guitarist Link Wray, a Dylan favorite, wrote a song with the sentence that opened each radio show, in the 1930s: "Only the shadow knows." The complete sentence was: "Who knows what evil lurks in the hearts of men? The Shadow knows!" followed by an ominous, threatening laugh and a musical theme, Camille Saint-Saëns' *Le Rouet d'Omphale* (*Omphale's Spinning Wheel*). The end of each episode reminded listeners, "Crime does not pay... The Shadow knows!" Radio shows frequently used such words as death, murder, devil, nightmare, and so on. All this combined with the needle, the skeleton, and the hanged man who vaguely resembles the then president of the U.S., Donald Trump, makes us think of the pandemic which hit America hard at the time.

The melody is drawn from a Billy 'The Kid' Emerson song, "If Lovin' Is Believin'," released in 1954 on the Sun Records label, with arrangements by Ike Turner. But this melody is a common blues, so Dylan modified it to make it more appealing: he changed the traditional twelve-bar structure to ten bars, and a bar was shortened from four to two times. It is the same Billy Emerson who wrote the song "Red Hot," covered by Billy Lee Riley, whom Dylan praised in his *Musicares* speech. Oddly enough, it is the third song in the album tuned to a C chord. Dylan's vindictive voice reminds us of "Early Roman Kings" and "Pay in Blood" on the album **Tempest**, and his way of phrasing of "My Wife's Hometown" on the album **Together Through Life**.

This song and the previous one, "I Contain Multitudes," are two Dylan songs where we can guess he openly talks of himself, which is a first time for such an artist, well-known to be very private.

The title "False Prophet" alludes to when Bob Dylan was invited by Pope John-Paul II, in September 1997 in Bologna, Italy. Pope Benedict XVI revealed he tried to stop Dylan from coming to this event, because he was afraid Dylan would make a false prophecy. John-Paul II gave a long sermon paraphrasing "Blowin' in the Wind," and saying the answer was Jesus Christ: "You ask me how many roads a man must walk down before he becomes a man. I answer: there is only one road for man, and it is the road of Jesus Christ, who said, 'I am the Way and the Life'."

As far as 1977, Dylan was using the term "false prophet" in a talk with Allen Ginsberg, about the film *Renaldo and Clara*. He read the Bible and was familiar with that term. It is actually in 1963 that Dylan used this term for the first time in one of his songs, "Long Time Gone," quoting the prophet Amos: "I was no prophet, neither was I a prophet's son." But in "False Prophet," Dylan does a double negation, "I *ain't no* false prophet," which could mean he is *not* a false prophet, or else he is a false prophet.

In 1985, in the TV show 20/20, Dylan said: "people can change things and make a difference... but there is a lot of false prophets around though. And... that's the trouble, people say they think they know what's right and other people they get people to follow them because they have a certain type of charisma. And there's always people willing to take over you know, people want a leader you know – and there'll be more and more of them."

Dylan was often called a prophet, but he kept denying it: "I never wanted to be a prophet or savior. Elvis maybe. I could easily see myself becoming him. But prophet? No." (Ed Bradley Interview, November 2004).

1	Another day that don't end, another ship going out
2	Another day of anger, bitterness and doubt
3	I know how it happened, I saw it begin
4	I opened my heart to the world, and the world came in

Line 4, "I opened my heart to the world, and the world came in" quotes the book *Awakening Osiris: A New Translation of the Egyptian Book of the Dead*, translated in everyday language, in 1989, by Normandi Ellis. The same book reads: "I cannot remember my birth and shall forget my death," which echoes to the song's last lines:

Can't remember when I was born
And I forgot when I died

Line 2 also draws from this book: "I know the names of the scorpions and they are these: anger, bitterness and doubt." The Egyptian Book of the Dead is a help for the passage from life to death, and for the multiple transformations between them, we find again the theme of ever changing. An important part of the song seems to be inspired by this book: a meditation on the constant fight between dark and light, good and evil, and the non-dualist nature of the being, sliding continuously between those poles, and between this life and the after-life.

Back to line 4, in the Bible, the "world" represents material life, opposed to spiritual life, and the prince of the world is none other than Satan. Dylan warned us against the "prince of the power of the air" in his 1979 song "Trouble." The apostle John told us that "many false prophets are gone out into the world," and the "antichrist already is in the world" (1 John 4:1-3).

In 2012, in an interview after the album **Tempest** release, Dylan said: "I believe in the Book of Revelation. I believe in disclosure, you know? There's truth in all books. In some kind of way. Confucius, [The Art of War by] Sun Tzu, [The Thoughts of] Marcus Aurelius, the Koran, the Torah, the New Testament, the Buddhist sutras, the Bhagavad-Gita, the Egyptian Book of the Dead, and many thousands more." Dylan took interest in ancient philosophies and religions a long time ago, as we can see in the lyrics of his songs "Isis" and "Jokerman."

This can be seen too in the *eye logo*, shown for years on a curtain at the back of his concert stages, and still on things for sale in his online store. The logo shows an eye, under a crown. The eye drawing is based on the udjat eye, or eye of Horus, the Egyptian falcon god. The myth tells us Horus, son of Isis and Osiris, lost an eye in the fight against his uncle Seth to avenge his father's killing. Seth tore off his eye, cut it in pieces and threw them in the Nile. Thoth picked up all the pieces except for one he added, and gave back to Horus his vital integrity. The eye combines the human eye and the falcon eye, it protects from illness and bad luck, and guides ships. It was painted on the ribbons of the mummies, to protect Pharaoh in the after-life.

This symbol can be found as well in Christian religion: "Behold, the eye of the Lord is upon them that fear him, upon them that hope in his mercy" (Psalms 33:18). It is the eye of Providence, or the eye of God which sees everything. In Mesopotamian civilizations, votive eyes are carved in stone, and named after the deity to which they are offered. The eye of God is also cast on Celtic coins. Its powers of seeing and hearing everything appear too in the three great monotheist religions – Jewish, Christian and Muslim. The Christians inscribe it sometimes in a triangle, symbol of the Trinity. It appears as well in Freemasonry, and as a synthesis between the Christian concepts and those of the Kabbalah.

Some interpret the eye as the god who is inside us, the permanent and internal truth. The crown above the eye would represent self-fulfillment, and the flame that goes out of the crown the illumination that happens when the truth has been found, when one reaches enlightenment, not merely knowledge.

Personally, I prefer to see it as a syncretic symbol, which combines several creeds, especially Dylan's Jewish origin and his acceptance of the New Testament, to which he added oriental and ancient creeds.

As an aside, Dylan played on the similar sounding of 'I' and 'eye', particularly in his song "I and I" – and also in his notes on the album *Highway 61 Revisited* back sleeve: "I cannot say the word eye any more... when I speak this word eye, it is as if I am speaking of somebody's eye that I faintly remember... there is no eye – there is only a series of mouths – long live the mouths."

We can find these ancient sources of inspiration in "Murder Most Foul" too, the line "They mutilated his body and they took out his brain," recalls the mummies preparation. Themes drawn from other creeds appear in the terms "Lord of the Gods," that is Indra in Hindu mythology. The "altar of the rising sun" may be Beijing Temple of the Sun, but there were temples of the sun for Hindu deities too, and Inca and Mayan and Japanese (Shinto) and ancient Egyptian religions.

In his song "I Contain Multitudes," the line "I sleep with life and death in the same bed" may refer to the ancient Egyptian belief that the soul could travel outside the body during sleep, and that it was a state close to death.

The picture of the Shadow accompanying "False Prophet" recalls ancient Egypt too, for the shadow was a living part of a person, one of the five states of the body. Back to Buddhism, the term "mountain of swords" (line 24) refers to the legend in the teaching of Buddha, saying a hermit had such a desire to know the truth he had to "climb a mountain of swords with bare feet."

As if by chance, the first modern writer who imagined a dialogue with a mummy was Edgar Allan Poe, in his story *Some Words with a Mummy*, in 1845.

5	Hello Mary Lou, hello Miss Pearl
6	My fleet footed guides from the underworld
7	No stars in the sky shine brighter than you
8	You girls mean business, and I do too
9	Well I'm the enemy of treason, the enemy of strife
10	I'm the enemy of the unlived, meaningless life
11	I ain't no false prophet, I just know what I know
12	I go where only the lonely can go

The narrator has two guides, Mary Lou and Miss Pearl, the former refers to the song "Hello Mary Lou" sung in 1961 by Ricky Nelson – Dylan covered Nelson's song "Lonesome Town" live in 1986 – the latter is a song by Jimmy Wages, recorded on the Sun label in 1957, and also alludes to Jimmie Rodgers' sister-in-law, Pearl Ella Pope Rodgers, who exercised a significant influence on him. Actually, Pearl can also allude to Peggy, as it is a diminutive for Margaret, which means Pearl in Greek. So, it makes us think of the Buddy Holly song "Peggy Sue." Buddy Holly was a big influence on the young Dylan, as stated in *Chronicles*: "Buddy was royalty, and I felt like she [Carolyn Hester] was my connection to it, to the rock-and-roll music that I'd played earlier, to that spirit." And at the beginning of his Nobel's lecture: "I felt related, like he [Buddy Holly] was an older brother. I even thought I resembled him. Buddy played the music that I loved – the music I grew up on: country and western, rock 'n' roll, and rhythm and blues." Pearl could also allude to Janis Joplin's nickname, as Bob met Janis not long before she died. In the Bible, the pearl illustrates the great value of the Kingdom of Heaven (Matthew 13:45-46).

Next line, Dylan refers to the Greek god Hermes and his winged sandals, and also to the "swift-footed" Achilles. Dylan sang it already in the 1964 song "Subterranean Homesick Blues," "Maggie comes fleet foot" – Maggie, another name for Pearl. In the Iliad, at the end of the Trojan war, Hermes is the god who enabled Ulysses to undertake the return trip to his home, Ithaca. And Achilles is a Trojan war hero, but he could not go home for he chose a short but glorious life, over a long "meaningless life," as in line 10. Hermes plays the role of the psychopomp – a conductor of souls into the afterlife. The two fleet-footed guides lead the narrator through the subterranean world, into the Underworld of Hades, like Orpheus.

Line 9 refers to Martin Luther's book *On the Freedom of a Christian*: "I am the *enemy of strife* and do not wish to incite or provoke anyone." Dylan always made it clear he did not want to lose his freedom for any religion.

13	I'm first among equals, second to none
14	The last of the best, you can bury the rest
15	Bury 'em naked with their silver and gold
16	Put 'em six feet under and I pray for their souls

"First among equals" alludes to the president of the Roman Senate, who was equal to the other senators. Augustus, the first Roman emperor, claimed he was, saying the Roman government was still a Republic, yet it was an Empire. The whole verse may read in reference to this statesman who became emperor by means of years of Civil war. "First among equals" was also used by the Christians, to mean a chief is elected among his equals, as the apostle Peter was chosen by Jesus Christ as the chief of the Church.

17	What are you lookin' at? There's nothin' to see
18	Just a cool breeze that's encircling me
19	Let's go for a walk in the garden, so far and so wide
20	We can sit in the shade by the fountain side
21	I search the world over for the Holy Grail
22	I sing songs of love, I sing songs of betrayal
23	Don't care what I drink, I don't care what I eat
24	I'll climb the mountain of swords on my bare feet
25	You don't know me darling, you never would guess
26	I'm not like my ghostly appearance would suggest
27	I ain't no false prophet, I just said what I said
28	I'm just here to bring vengeance on somebody's head

29	Put out your hand, there's nothin' to hold
30	Open your mouth, I'll stuff it with gold
31	Aw, you poor devil, look up if you will
32	The City of God is up there on the hill

Line 19, the garden may allude to the Garden of Eden and the temptation of the "world," as in line 4.

Line 21, the narrator searches for the Holy Grail, just like Indiana Jones in the 1989 film *Indiana Jones and The Last Crusade*.

"Open your mouth, I'll stuff it with gold" refers once more to the Ancient Romans: Crassus was a general and politician and the richest man in Rome, but he was defeated by the Parthians in 53 BC, and they poured molten gold into his mouth in symbolic mockery of his thirst for wealth. Is this a metaphor for our consumer's world? The Roman poet Ovid mentioned Crassus several times in his works, and Dylan quoted Ovid's lines in a few songs in his last albums, particularly "Ain't Talkin'."

Line 32, *The City of God* is a book of Christian philosophy written by Augustine of Hippo in the early 5th century AD. It represents the opposite of the "world" named in line 4. Dylan knew Augustine by the late 1960s, as he sang in "I Dreamed I Saw St. Augustine," released in the album **John Wesley Harding**. This term may also refer to the "city upon a hill" which was supposed to describe the settling of people in America, according to John Winthrop in his sermon, *A Model of Christian Charity*.

33	Hello stranger, hello and goodbye
34	You rule the land, but so do I
35	You lusty old mule, you got a poison brain
36	I'll marry you to a ball and chain
37	You know darlin', the kinda life that I live
38	When your smile meets my smile, somethin' has got to give
39	I ain't no false prophet, nah, I'm nobody's bride
40	Can't remember when I was born, and I forgot when I died

As in the two previous songs in this essay, Dylan refers to more or less famous songs. Line 12, "Only the Lonely" is a well-known song by Roy Orbison, who sang and played with Bob in the super-group The Traveling Wilburys. Dylan played guitar on this song in February 1990, at a tribute concert to Roy Orbison after his death.

Line 33, "Hello Stranger" was sung by the Carter Family, a group that inspired Woody Guthrie among many others, and whose photograph is on the album sleeve. "Hello and goodbye" may be another reference to The Beatles, to their 1967 song "Hello, Goodbye." The song "Long Goodbye" was sung in 1973 by Clydie King, in the film of the same name, directed by Robert Altman, based on the hard-boiled detective novel by Raymond Chandler. Clydie did backup vocals for Bob Dylan on several tours, and some say they were secretly married and had two children. When she died in January 2019, Dylan said: "She was my ultimate singing partner. No one ever came close. We were two soulmates."

Line 36, several songs are named "Ball and Chain." Dylan most likely thinks of the song written by Rythm'n'Blues singer Big Mama Thornton, covered in the late 1960s by Janis Joplin.

Line 35, "lusty old mule" can be found in Homer's Iliad, line 663.

Line 38, *Something's Got to Give* is the last film Marylin Monroe acted in. Its screenplay is a mix of comedy and noir story, but it was unfinished due to Marylin's death on August 4, 1962.

The last line may be inspired from the Bhagavad-Gita, one of the holy scriptures of Hinduism: "The Spirit was not born; It will never die, nor once having been, can It cease to be. Unborn, Eternal, Ever-enduring, yet Most Ancient, the Spirit dies not when the body is dead."

"False Prophet" belongs to the same family as the two other songs previously available. It draws on the same themes and sources of inspiration, only more aggressive and humorous. Dylan mixes ancient and modern, secular and holy, classical and popular references, asking his listeners to understand he is neither prophet, nor false prophet. He puts forward in a concealed way some of his ideas about life and the present state of the world. At the same time, he uses irony in a stronger way than in his two previous songs, as if to say all of that is not really important, and his time left living would not be enough to persuade his contemporaries, if he wanted to. Bob Dylan said so sixty years ago, in more simple and direct terms:

If I can't help somebody
With a word or song,
If I can't show somebody
They are travelin' wrong.
But I know I ain't no prophet
An' I ain't no prophet's son.
I'm just a long time a-comin'
An' I'll be a long time gone.
  ("Long Time Gone", 1963).

5 - My Own Version of You

"My Own Version of You" makes us think right away of Mary Shelley's novel, *Frankenstein; or, The Modern Prometheus*. The original version of this well-known novel, published in 1818, tells the story of a scientist who creates life and is terrified by what he did. But in Bob Dylan's revisited version, only the preliminary steps are told, the way of making "my own version of you."

It may also allude to "I Put a Spell on You" by Screamin' Jay Hawkins, covered by Nina Simone and hundreds other artists. On stage, Hawkins wore a long cape, and rose out of a coffin in the midst of smoke and fog. This theatrical act was one of the first shock rock performances.

The melody is a swift waltz, with suspended effects evoking crime noir or detective films. We recognize the chords from the James Bond film theme, *On Her Majesty's Secret Service.*

1	All through the summers into January
2	I've been visiting morgues and monasteries
3	Lookin' for the necessary body parts
4	Limbs and livers and brains and hearts
5	I'll bring someone to life is what I wanna do
6	I wanna create my own version of you

First verse exposes the narrator's aim, create my own version of you, but who is "you?" Could it be the creation of Bob Dylan by Robert Zimmerman? Or the process of creating his own songs? Dylan paraphrases the first lines of "Sitting on Top of the World," written and sung by one of his favorite groups, The Mississippi Sheiks. In the 1990s, he covered two songs written by this group, "Blood in My Eyes" in his album **World Gone Wrong**, and "Sitting on Top of the World" in his album **Good as I Been to You**. Nowadays he is inspired again by the latter: "Was all the summer, and all the fall/ Just trying to find my little all in all" is a lot like "All through the summers into January … Lookin' for the necessary body parts." The narrator looks for body parts, liver especially. It recalls the myth of Prometheus, the titan who stole the fire to give it to humanity, thus creating civilization, and who in return was punished by Zeus, king of the Olympian gods: he was bound to a rock, and an eagle – the emblem of Zeus – was sent to eat his liver, that grew back overnight.

7	Well, it must be the winter of my discontent
8	I wish you'd have taken me with you wherever you went
9	They talk all night, and they talk all day
10	Not for a minute do I believe anything they say
11	I'm going to make some other life, someone I've never seen
12	You know what I mean, you know exactly what I mean

Line 7 is based on Shakespeare's "the winter of our discontent," the first line of the play Richard III. It was also the title of John Steinbeck's last novel, which got him the 1962 Nobel Prize in Literature. This novel addresses the moral degeneration of American culture during the 1950s and 1960s, a good reason for Dylan to refer to this book. Shakespeare is quoted another time, line 49, with Hamlet's famous question, "to be or not to be?"

From the beginning of the song, those persons dissecting his songs, talking "all night and all day," "not for a minute [does he] believe anything they say," who are they supposed to be, if not the fans and critics? It is the winter of his discontent, he wishes they would have taken him along, that they would try to understand him. Further on (line 22 and 42), he talks of "someone who feels the way that I feel," and adds "I'm not gonna get involved in any insignificant details," two more barbs against those people.

Although we do not claim to exhaust the subject, Bob Dylan's relations with his fans and with reporters always were equivocal. In numerous interviews, he rejects them and says he does not care about their opinions, and at most of his shows he runs out of the stage right after the last salute, to escape people who would like to speak to him or have him sign autographs. All the same, he rarely pays attention to the things thrown at him on the stage, even flowers, and hardly ever takes any present from his admirers. Such an attitude can be understood, when one knows he has been harassed by fans, some going so far as coming into his house, particularly a fake Ms. Sara Dylan, who waited for him at every hotel on tour. Besides he was scared of getting killed by a fan, especially after John Lennon's murder. Yet, there have been occasions where he was nice to his fans, chatting with them and signing autographs. On a few tours he happened to leave dozens of persons to climb on the stage, or he signaled his bodyguard to allow somebody getting closer to him. But old age is wearing on him, and contacts with fans get rarer and rarer.

With the critics and journalists, there was a time in 1965-66 when he systematically made fun of them, it should be said they assailed him with stupid questions, e.g. – Journalist: "Does it take a lot of trouble to get your hair like that?", "How do you feel about selling out?", "How many folk singers are there now?" Dylan: "No, you just have to sleep on it for about twenty years," "I don't feel guilt," "136" respectively. Afterwards, he was rather cooperative in his interviews, even though he might answer by a single word, or ignore the question. Dylan says he disregards critics, but his close friends say he often reads them, and is pissed off when they are bad, when they do not even try to understand what he does. This is no more a problem since in the latest years nearly all critics are laudatory, maybe too much. In short, like any person who has been famous for such a long time, Bob Dylan protects himself from unknown people, and will not be influenced by people who think they know him and his music better than himself. On top of this, he knows he has not so many years left to live, and he already had knowledge of a multitude of things and met a multitude of people.

13	I'll take the Scarface Pacino and the Godfather Brando
14	Mix it up in a tank and get a robot commando
15	If I do it up right and put the head on straight
16	I'll be saved by the creature that I create

Line 13, the narrator, or Dylan disguised as Frankenstein, mentions two famous actors in their roles as criminals.

Next line, he alludes to the Robot Commando, a 19" tall toy, released in 1961, that was marketed as a "one-man army."

Line 16 could have several meanings. It makes us think of the original novel, in which the scientist Frankenstein fears his creature will destroy him, or it may be Bob Dylan who will be saved by his creation of himself, or else by the creation of his songs.

17	I'll get blood from a cactus, gunpowder from ice
18	I don't gamble with cards, and I don't shoot no dice
19	If you look at my face with your sightless eye
20	Can you cross your heart and hope to die
21	I'll bring someone to life, someone for real
22	Someone who feels the way that I feel

Line 17, the narrator evokes the cochineal, an insect that lives in cactuses and gives them a blood-colored dye. Then he quotes *Gulliver's Travels* by Jonathan Swift, in which a man is at work to "calcine ice into gunpowder."

23	I study Sanskrit and Arabic to improve my mind
24	I want to do things for the benefit of all mankind
25	I say to the willow tree, don't weep for me
26	I'm saying to hell to all things that used to be

The beginning of the fifth verse is widely based on the novel *Frankenstein*, that takes an interest in the cultures at the origin of occidental civilization, Sanskrit and Arabic, and Greek and Roman poetry, and prefers understanding over criticizing. These themes can be found in other Dylan songs. At the same time, Dylan tells us he still likes to "improve his mind" with more knowledge.

As noted by Richard F. Thomas, Professor of Classical Literature at Harvard, line 24 paraphrases a line in Roman poet Virgil's Aeneid, that follows the line carved on the Nobel prize medal. In that work, there is a scene describing the Elysian Fields, containing the sentence carved on the medal (see chapter 6, "Mother of Muses"), and next line evokes those "we remember well for the good they did mankind," which is similar to "do things for the benefit of all mankind."

Line 25 refers to a jazz standard sung by Billie Holiday and Nina Simone, "Willow Weep for Me."

27	Well I get into trouble, then I hit the wall
28	No place to turn, no place at all
29	I pick a number between one and two
30	And I ask myself what would Julius Caesar do
31	I will bring someone to life, in more ways than one
32	Don't matter how long it takes, it'll be done when it's done
33	I'm gonna make you play the piano like Leon Russell
34	Like Liberace, like St. John the Apostle
35	I'll play every number that I can play
36	I'll see you maybe on Judgment Day

Line 30, the song mentions once more a Roman leader, Julius Caesar, or maybe it alludes to Jesus Christ who was brought back to life. The initials are the same.

Line 33 likely refers to the piano player machines that were popular in the nineteenth century, around the same time as *Frankenstein*, and as Offenbach, a composer whose tune Dylan borrowed for the next song, "I've Made Up My Mind to Give Myself to You." Offenbach's plays were inspired by E.T.A. Hoffman's novels, especially *The Sandman*, in which he mentioned an "automaton."

One wonders why the apostle Saint John comes after the pianists Leon Russell – a musician who played with The Rolling Stones, Joe Cocker, and Dylan in 1971 at the Bangladesh concert – and Liberace – a flamboyant concert pianist. Dylan may think of the song "John the Revelator," a famous gospel tune based on the book of Revelation, written by John of Patmos, whom most consider to be John the Apostle.

37	After midnight if you still want to meet
38	I'll be at the Black Horse tavern on Armageddon Street
39	Two doors down, not that far to walk
40	I'll hear your footsteps, you won't have to knock
41	I'll bring someone to life, balance the scales
42	I'm not gonna get involved in any insignificant details
43	You can bring it to St. Peter, you can bring it to Jerome
44	You can bring it all the way over, bring it all the way home
45	Bring it to the corner, where the children play
46	You can bring it to me on a silver tray
47	I'll bring someone to life, spare no expense
48	Do it with decency and common sense
49	Can you tell me what it means, to be or not to be
50	You won't get away with foolin' me
51	Can you help me walk that moonlight mile
52	Can you give me the blessings of your smile
53	I'll bring someone to life, use all of my powers
54	Do it in the dark, in the wee, small hours
55	I can see the history of the whole human race
56	It's all right there, it's carved into your face
57	Should I break it all down, should I fall on my knees
58	Is there light at the end of the tunnel, can you tell me please

Line 38, the Black Horse Tavern makes us think of the White Horse Tavern, where Dylan Thomas used to go in the 1950s, and where Bob Dylan spent many nights the first years he was in New York. There he listened to the Irish group the Clancy Brothers, and to Tommy Makem, whom he mentions in

Chronicles. The narrator changes white to black, it is a gloomy sign, indeed black was the color of the horse of the third horseman in the Book of Revelation. On the other hand, a Black Horse Tavern was built in 1812 in Gettysburg, Pennsylvania, and its mill tract was used as a field hospital in the Battle of Gettysburg. The Armageddon is the prophesied location of a gathering of armies for a battle during the end times, referring to the Book of Revelation in the New Testament, the Quran, and in popular culture. Dylan already used this term in two of his songs, "Señor" and "Are You Ready."

Line 43 on, Dylan plays on the double meaning of *bring*: its usual meaning is like *take* or *come up with*, but *bring to life* may mean *cause to regain consciousness or return as if from death* (Oxford Dictionary). It asks again the question, what does the narrator bring, who or what is brought to life? Could it be a metaphor for artistic creation? Dylan could be describing his techniques of writing, e.g. to bring life to his songs, he takes crumbs of texts and real or fictional, and to "mix [them] up in a tank" (line 13).

"Bring It to Jerome" was sung in 1958 by Bo Diddley, a black rocker who sang the well-known songs "Not Fade Away" and "Who Do You Love." Dylan sang "Not Fade Away" over a hundred times on tour, as an encore most of the time.

Saint Jerome translated the Bible from Hebrew and Greek to Latin, and so is the patron saint of translators. He lived an ascetic life, although his family was rich. Saint Peter is the first among equals, as referred in "False Prophet."

Line 44 may refer to Dylan's fourth album, ***Bringing It All Back Home***.

Line 46, the "silver tray" alludes most likely to John the Baptist, whose head was delivered to Salome on a silver platter, as pictured on many paintings.

Line 47 may allude to the 1993 film *Jurassic Park*, that is a similar story to Frankenstein's, only they bring life back to dinosaurs. While creating the park of dinosaurs, the businessman John Hammond keeps saying "spare no expense."

Then Dylan mentions the Rolling Stones song, "Moonlight Mile," and a bit further, one of Frank Sinatra's best albums, released in 1955, *In the Wee Small Hours*, whose general mood was of sadness and irony.

Line 49 puts Shakespeare's famous question in a different context, giving it a new meaning.

59	Stand over there by the cypress tree
60	Where the Trojan women and children are sold into slavery
61	Long before the first crusade
62	Way back 'fore England or America were made
63	Step right into the burning hell
64	Where some of the best-known enemies of mankind dwell
65	Mr. Freud with his dreams, Mr. Marx with his axe
66	See the rawhide lash rip the skin from their backs
67	Got the right spirit, you can feel it, you can hear it
68	You've got what they call the immortal spirit
69	You can feel it all night, you can feel it in the morn'
70	It creeps in your body the day you are born
71	One strike of lightning is all that I need
72	And a blast of 'lectricity that runs at top speed
73	Shimmy your ribs, I'll stick in the knife
74	Gonna jump-start my creation to life
75	I wanna bring someone to life, turn back the years
76	Do it with laughter and do it with tears

Lines 59-62 refer again to Virgil's Aeneid: The "cypress tree" is the place where Aeneas asks his family to wait for him, and a bit further in the same book II, *The Fall of Troy*, the poet mentions Trojan women and children. It happened indeed "long before the first crusade."

Line 65, Freud was known for his analysis of dreams, and Marx's project was to create a new society that would put the present one in the museum, next to the bronze ax.

Lines 71-72 recall the first film about Frankenstein, released in 1931, where they used electricity from a storm to bring the creature to life.

Last line, laughter and tears are two things only human beings can do.

———————————————

The song begins on a somewhat luminous note, with a resolution to create life, but it becomes dark and frightening, with descending musical chords. The use of negative words – black, dark, Armageddon, break down, tunnel, cypress, hell, creep, lightning, tears – and sinister phrases, increase more and more. All this produces a gothic horror mood, as in Mary Shelley's novel.

Mary Shelley was born in 1797. Her mother was a feminist philosopher, writer and teacher, Mary Wollstonecraft, and her father a philosopher, novelist and journalist, William Godwin. Thanks to him, she had an exceptional education for a girl at the time. She could read books on Greek and Roman history, and meet highly cultured relations, the poet Coleridge and a former U.S. Vice-President, Aaron Burr, among others.

At 16, she met the poet and anarchist philosopher Percy Shelley, who was 21, and flew to France with him. They went back to Great Britain, where she bore him a child, but lost the child at a young age, and that probably influenced her first novel's topic. Later she had another child, and the three of them went to Switzerland to stay with the romantic poet, Byron. It is where she wrote *Frankenstein*, in June 1816, following a discussion on experiences with electricity, that would make it possible to bring life back to a corpse. After a stay in Italy, she came back to London with her child, in 1822, when Percy Shelley died. There she went on writing and published several novels, while supporting radical ideas, and defending the cause of women, free love and homosexuality, in her novels and essays as well as in her life.

Doctor Frankenstein could be viewed as poet John Milton's Satan, in his major work *Paradise Lost*: He rebels against tradition to create life, he decides on his destiny, but this ambition is actually an illusion, masked as a search for truth. Mary Shelley thought society could improve, as taught by the Enlightenment doctrine, but she feared that the exercise of power in an irresponsible way would lead to chaos. She was pessimistic about human nature. "My Own Version of You" can be viewed in the same way, like the history of the creation by Satan, a parody of the creation by God. In particular the line "What would Julius Caesar do?" can be seen as a parody of Jesus Christ. References to Freud and Marx confirm this idea, for they are two personalities whose works contributed to the alienation of God from the human life, in science and politics respectively.

With this perspective, Dylan wrote a tribute to Mary Shelley, a free woman who was one of the first famous female writers, and the hidden meaning of the song would be a dylanesque version of her famous novel.

But at the same time, Dylan is mocking us, who want to give a hidden meaning to each of his words, and mocking himself, who sometimes thought he was The Creator, while his creation was simply made from "pieces" of other works he put together and transformed, until he created his own version of him.

6 - I've Made Up My Mind to Give Myself to You

"I've made up my mind" is the line opening the song "I Can't Stop Loving You," a big hit by Ray Charles in 1962. "I Can't Stop Loving You" relates well with the theme of this Dylan song, and the chorus, "I'll just live my life of dreams of yesterday," resounds like one of the greater impressions given by the album **Rough and Rowdy Ways**.

The melody is a barcarole, that is a three-time bar, at 6/8 meter, which evokes the slow moving of a bark. This tune was originally sung by Venetian gondoliers, then became fashionable in the eighteenth and nineteenth centuries. Actually, it is one of the most famous barcaroles, "Belle nuit, ô nuit d'amour," ("Beautiful Night, Oh Night of Love"), composed by Jules Barbier and Jacques Offenbach for the *opéra fantastique The Tales of Hoffman*, in 1881, used in several films. Dylan covered a piece of Offenbach's work in his 1990 tour, as an instrumental. Dylan's lyrics share themes with *The Tales of Hoffman*, both referring to night and melancholy.

It is sung magnificently, with backing vocals. It is the album's song that is the most influenced by Dylan's singing of the Great American Songbook.

1	I'm sitting on my terrace, lost in the stars
2	Listening to the sounds of the sad guitars
3	Been thinking it all over, and I thought it all through
4	I've made up my mind to give myself to you
5	I saw the first fall of snow
6	I saw the flowers come and go
7	I don't think that anyone ever else ever knew
8	I've made up my mind to give myself to you

Once more, the *You* in the song's title is hard to identify. In the sixth verse, the narrator talks to a man: "You're a traveling man." It seems Dylan talks from a woman's point of view, but at the end of the same verse, he writes "I'm going far away from home with her," so it must be a man talking. Likewise in the last verse, "I knew you'd say yes," it is unlikely a man would say that, unless he is full of himself. It would not be the first time Dylan takes a woman's point of view; the 1964 song "North Country Blues" is another example.

Line 5, "At the First Fall of Snow" is a Hank Williams song recorded in 1947. He was the first Country singer to be as popular as a rock star, and one of Dylan's "first idols." Line 6 recalls Pete Seeger's song "Where Have All the Flowers Gone," an anti-war hymn that was very popular in the early 1960s. These two songs expressed the loss of the innocence.

9	I'm giving myself to you, I am
10	From Salt Lake City to Birmingham
11	From East LA to San Antone
12	I don't think I could bear to live my life alone
13	My eye is like a shooting star
14	It looks at nothing here or there, looks at nothing near or far
15	No one ever told me, it's just something I knew
16	I've made up my mind to give myself to you
17	If I had the wings of a snow-white dove

18	I'd preach the gospel, the gospel of love
19	A love so real, a love so true
20	I've made up my mind to give myself to you
21	Take me out traveling, you're a traveling man
22	Show me something that I'll understand
23	I'm not what I was, things aren't what they were
24	I'm going far away from home with her
25	I traveled the long road of despair
26	I've met no other traveler there
27	Lotta people gone, a lotta people I knew
28	I've made up my mind to give myself to you
29	Well, my heart's like a river, a river that sings
30	Just takes me a while to realize things
31	I'll see you at sunrise, I'll see you at dawn
32	I'll lay down beside you when everyone's gone
33	I traveled from the mountains to the sea
34	I hope that the gods go easy with me
35	I knew you'd say yes, I'm saying it too
36	I've made up my mind to give myself to you

Line 17, "Wings of a Dove" is a 1958 Country song, that alludes to the Bible scene where God sent a dove to Noah (Genesis 8:6-12), and also to the gospel according to Matthew (3:16), when Jesus was baptized: "he saw the Spirit of God descending like a dove, and lighting upon him." Hence the next line talks of preaching the gospel, as Dylan did from 1979 to 1981, in his records and on tour.

Line 21, "Travelin' Man" is a 1961 song by Ricky Nelson. At the beginning of *Chronicles*, Dylan remembers hearing this song at the Cafe Wha, during his first winter in New York, and how he "felt kin to him [Ricky Nelson]," and it strengthened his desire to play and record his music. This "traveling man" evokes as well the American singer Johnny Cash, who spent his life on the road, to play his music and to run away from his problems. Johnny Cash wrote to Bob Dylan in 1963, saying he liked his second album, ***The Freewheelin' Bob Dylan***. Dylan was happy and honored to receive a letter from such a famous musician. They met in New York, at the Gaslight, then at the 1964 Newport Festival. Dylan offered two songs to Cash, "It Ain't Me Babe" and "Mama You Been on My Mind," in return Cash gave him his guitar. When Dylan was criticized for his "dropping the protest songs," Cash supported him and wrote to the folk magazine *Broadside*: "Shut up and let the boy sing!" They met again in 1966 in London, as the film *Eat the Document* includes a scene where they duetted. Then in 1969 they recorded several songs together, the most well-known being a new version of "Girl from the North Country," released on the album ***Nashville Skyline***. The complete session was released in 2019 in compilations. Dylan gave to Cash his song "Wanted Man," which he never sang afterwards. Cash died in 2003, and Dylan paid tribute to him: "Cash Is King. In plain terms, Johnny was and is the North Star; you could guide your ship by him."

Travel was the topic of numerous Cash songs – "Wayfaring Stranger," "The Wayworn Traveler," "Sing a Travelin' Song," "I've Been Everywhere." What's more, the lines *"give myself to you"* and *"lay with me"* from "I've Made Up My Mind to Give Myself to You" can be found in the Johnny Cash song "Would You Lay with Me (In a Field of Stone)."

In short, Bob Dylan most likely thought of Johnny Cash while writing his song, in addition to Ricky Nelson.

At the same time, the song's framework seems to be inspired by the Charles Dickens novel, *A Tale of Two Cities*. The character of Mr. Stryver acts in the same way as in a few lines in Dylan's song: "No one ever told me, it's just something I knew," "I knew you'd say yes," and the two Dickens cities, London and Paris, could be replaced by Los Angeles and San Antonio, especially since the Parisian quarter *Saint-Antoine* is one of the key places in the novel's action.

Once more, Dylan mixes several sources of inspiration and creates a unique and personal song. But it is not enough to give a meaning to the song. Back to our first idea, this song is a dialogue with a woman, the poet's muse. At the beginning, the muse thinks on her own, she is ready to give herself to the poet, but he does not know it yet. From line 21 onwards, the muse definitely decided to give herself to the poet, and he is now ready:

> Take me out traveling, you're a traveling man
> Show me something that I'll understand

He speaks to another person:

> I'm not what I was, things aren't what they were
> I'm going far away from home with her

I am not what I was, inspiration does not come easy any more, I am going away with my muse. The seventh verse continues the poet's complaint, who traveled a lot and met no one, and who would like to lay with his muse now she seems to want it. The muse answers she traveled much as well, and she knew he would say yes.

7 - Black Rider

At first look, the "Black Rider" makes us think of death, and of the Book of Revelation – the Third Horseman of the Apocalypse – especially when you know Bob Dylan often refers to the Bible, but it may not be that simple, this song's lyrics do not fit with this idea.

Dylan sings slowly and enunciates each word, which we are not accustomed to. The melody seems simple, but according to the Bob Dylan fan and musicologist Eyolf Oestrem, it is one of the most complicated of Dylan's songs, for its chord chart defies all expectations.

The title "Black Rider" had been used for a Bob Wills song, released in 1938 with his Western Swing group Bob Wills and His Texas Playboys.

The same title was also used in 1990 by Tom Waits, William Burroughs and Robert Wilson in an opera. In this case, the Black Rider was the devil. This opera's subtitle is "The Casting of the Magic Bullets," which recalls the theory of the "magic bullet" that killed President Kennedy.

Lastly, this title refers to Stephen Crane's poems: *Black Riders & Other Lines*. It is most likely the origin of the Dylan song title, for he mentions Crane in *Chronicles*. Dylan met Archibald MacLeish in 1969. He asked Bob to write songs for a theater play he was writing. It did not happen and the Dylan songs ended up in the album **New Morning**, but MacLeish "told me some remarkable stuff about the novelist Stephen Crane, who wrote *The Red Badge of Courage*. He said he was a sickly reporter always on the side of the underdog. He didn't go to cocktail parties or theater openings – went to Cuba to cover the Cuban War, drank a lot and died of tuberculosis at twenty-eight. It sounded like Crane was the Robert Johnson of literature. Jimmie Rodgers died of TB, too. I wondered if they ever crossed paths."

Black Riders & Other Lines contains 68 poems and was published in May 1895, when Crane was 23. It caused a scandal at the time for the poems were in an unconventional style, and questioned the existence of God. Actually, these poems were mainly inspired by the Bible – Crane's father was a well-known minister who brought his children up in his religion – but at the same time they rejected God and religion. A few months later, Crane published his novel *The Red Badge of Courage*, the story of a young private in the Union Army, who flees from the field of battle. Overcome with shame, he longs for a wound, a "red badge of courage," to counteract his cowardice. This novel became a best seller, but Crane himself thought *The Black Riders* a superior work. As he wrote, "the former is the more ambitious effort. In it, I am to give my ideas of life as a whole, so far as I know it, and the latter [*The Red Badge of Courage*] is a mere episode – an amplification."

In the first poem, the one that gave its name to the collection, *"Black Riders came from the sea,"* as in the song "'Cross the Green Mountain," released in 2002.

1	Black rider, black rider, you been living too hard
2	Been up all night, have to stay on your guard
3	The path that you're walking, too narrow to walk
4	Every step of the way, another stumbling block
5	The road that you're on, same road that you know
6	Just not the same as it was a minute ago

Line 3 mentions a narrow path, as in the song "Narrow Way" on the album *Tempest*. It refers to the Bible (Matthew 7:14): "Because strait is the gate, and narrow is the way, which leadeth unto life, and few there be that find it."

Line 4 recalls the songs "Murder Most Foul," "I Contain Multitudes" and "False Prophet" (Matthew 7:15): "Beware of *false prophets*, which come to you in sheep's clothing, but inwardly they are ravening *wolves*."

Line 5-6 may refer to Heraclites' philosophy, the road changes but stays the same, as in "I Contain Multitudes."

7	Black rider, black rider, you've seen it all
8	You've seen the great world and you've seen the small
9	You fell into the fire and you're eating the flame
10	Better seal up your lips if you want to stay in the game
11	Be reasonable mister, be honest, be fair
12	Let all of your earthly thoughts be of prayer

Line 8, the "great world and (...) the small" may allude to the Taoist religion:

Great knowledge is broad and encompassing
Small knowledge is detailed and meticulous
Great talk is powerful and forceful
Small talk is endless and argumentative

In this oriental philosophy, the great world is the world of wisdom, bravery, and virtue, while the small world is characterized by pettiness and critique.

Line 10, the sealed lips are inspired by prophet Isaiah, when an angel touched Isaiah's lips with a burning coal, thus purifying his words (Isaiah 6:6-7).

13	Black rider, black rider, all dressed in black
14	I'm walking away, you try to make me look back
15	My heart is at rest, I'd like to keep it that way
16	I don't want to fight at least not today
17	Go home to your wife, stop visiting mine
18	One of these days I'll forget to be kind

Line 14, "you try to make me look back" makes us think of Lot's wife, who was told to flee the wickedness of Sodom and not to look back and was turned into a pillar of salt upon ignoring the angel's orders (Genesis 19:26). Lines 17-18 refer to adultery and "forget to be kind" allude to the Bible as well (Hebrews 13:2-4).

19	Black rider, black rider, tell me when, tell me how
20	If there ever was a time, then let it be now
21	Let me go through, open the door
22	My soul is distressed, my mind is at war
23	Don't hug me, don't flatter me, don't turn on the charm
24	I take a sword and hack off your arm
25	Black rider, black rider, hold it right there
26	The size of your cock won't get you nowhere
27	I suffer in silence, I'll not make a sound
28	Maybe I'll take the high moral ground
29	Some enchanted evening, I'll sing you a song
30	Black rider, black rider, you've been on the job too long

Now for something different, line 26 is drawn from the *Satires* by ancient Rome poet Juvenal, whom Dylan already quoted in his song "Tempest." It must come from an ancient author for Dylan to allow himself such coarse words.

"Some Enchanted Evening" is a song written in 1949 by Rodgers and Hammerstein, for the musical *South Pacific*. It was covered by many artists, Frank Sinatra of course, and Dylan in his album **Shadows in the Night**. It tells the story of the passionate love of a soldier for a nurse.

"He been on the job too long" is the refrain of the song "Duncan and Brady," recorded for the first time in 1929. This murder ballad tells of the killing of a policeman, Brady, by a bartender, Duncan. It was sung by Leadbelly, a noted influence on Bobby Zimmerman, and Dave Van Ronk, one of Dylan's best friends in Greenwich Village. "Duncan and Brady" was recorded in a studio session by Dylan in June 1992, with David Bromberg, for an album that was not released. Two tracks were released in the 2008 Bootleg Series Vol.8, this one and a Jimmie Rodgers' cover, "Miss the Mississippi and You." Dylan played "Duncan and Brady" live in the 1999 and 2000 tours, often opening his shows. This song includes the line "Gonna shoot somebody jus' to watch him die," used by Johnny Cash in his famous song "Folsom Prison Blues." Cash spent most of his life "all dressed in black," and it became his surname: "The Man in Black." In 1971 he wrote a song with that name explaining why. The song was a protest statement against the treatment of poor people by wealthy politicians, mass incarceration, and "for the thousands who have died."

So, who is this Black Rider the narrator is talking to? It could be Bob Dylan talking to himself, thinking of mortality, his own and that of his friends, and how old age makes life harder. The narrator tries to accept this fact he cannot dodge, with prayers and philosophic thoughts, but cannot help but rebel and threaten. He ends on an ironic line, enchanting the Black Rider with a song, in hope he grants him a grace period. The lyrics of "Black Rider" compare with the famous John Donne poem, "Death Be Not Proud." This poem challenges the power of death, saying it is subject to other forces such as "fate, chance, kings, and desperate men," that its power is less strong than drugs, and that "Death shalt die." As Bob Dylan sang, it has "been on the job too long."

8 - Goodbye Jimmy Reed

Jimmy Reed began to play the blues after the second world war, he had his first big hit in 1957 with "Honest I Do," then "Baby What You Want Me to Do," "Ain't That Lovin' You Baby," "Big Boss Man," "Bright Lights, Big City," and so on. His songs were covered by numerous musicians, such as Elvis Presley, The Rolling Stones, Eric Clapton, Eric Burdon, The Grateful Dead, Neil Young, Jimi Hendrix. Bob Dylan named his song "Odds and Ends" – in *The Basement Tapes* – after a Jimmy Reed song, and possibly borrowed its tune.

The melody of "Goodbye Jimmy Reed" is a blues-rock, borrowed from "Down in Virginia," a song Jimmy Reed recorded in 1958, whose title Dylan mentions at the end of his song.

1	I live on a street named after a saint
2	Women in the churches wear powder and paint
3	Where the Jews and the Catholics and the Muslims all pray
4	I can tell a Proddy from a mile away
5	Goodbye Jimmy Reed, Jimmy Reed indeed
6	Give me that old time religion, it's just what I need
7	For thine is the kingdom, the power and the glory
8	Go tell it on the mountain, go tell the real story
9	Tell it in that straightforward puritanical tone
10	In the mystic hours when a person's alone
11	Goodbye Jimmy Reed, God speed
12	Thump on the bible, proclaim a creed
13	You won't amount to much the people all said

14	'Cos I didn't play guitar behind my head
15	Never pandered, never acted proud
16	Never took off my shoes, threw 'em into the crowd
17	Goodbye Jimmy Reed, goodbye and good night
18	Put a jewel in your crown and I'll put out the light

At first glance, the lyrics of "Goodbye Jimmy Reed" have little to do with Jimmy Reed. We cannot help thinking it is similar to the song "Blind Willie McTell," that is named after an early twentieth century bluesman, but whose lyrics do not *directly* concern Blind Willie McTell's life, for they are mainly about slavery and racism.

In the same way, one can ask why Dylan did not name this song after the Northern Irish Van Morrison, for it refers to him so many times. If we look into Van Morrison's biography by Johnny Rogan, *Van Morrison: No Surrender*, we can find several more or less obvious matches with the lyrics of "Goodbye Jimmy Reed."

The most obvious reference is this book's chapter titled "Are You a Proddy?", in which Rogan writes that comedian Spike Milligan, himself an Irish Catholic, asked Morrison that question. Van Morrison was born in a protestant family, even though later on he undertook a spiritual quest, exploring various wisdoms, sects and religions, especially oriental philosophies. He finally stuck to *No Guru, No Method, No Teacher* (name of his sixteenth album), and "No Religion" (a song from his twenty-third album, *Days Like This*), a process close to Dylan's. The term "Proddy" is used by Irish Catholics to denigrate Protestants, and it is most unlikely Dylan used it in his song without thinking of his highly-regarded friend. Also, the sentence "you could tell by looking at somebody if they were a

Protestant," at the beginning of this biography, looks much like Dylan's line, "I can tell a Proddy from a mile away."

At least six matches can be counted in the fifty first pages of this biography. The song's first line looks like those lines from the book: "Catholics all went to schools named after saints and Protestants went to schools named after streets." As noted by Rogan, the line "For thine is the kingdom, the power and the glory" refers to the Lord's prayer; this prayer is known to all Christians, but when Van Morrison was young, this line was spoken only by Protestants. Line 9, the word "puritanical" alludes to Van's upbringings. Line 14 alludes to the guitar players in The Monarchs who played with their guitars behind their heads, a trick they took from the bluesmen, particularly Charley Patton, whose name Dylan used in a song title, "High Water (for Charley Patton)." Line 16 alludes to "the famous Morrison trick of taking his shoes off on stage," as reported by Rogan. Line 18, "jewel in your crown" alludes to Rogan's line about Van Morrison's school, "Orangefield regarded as the *jewel in the crown*." On the other hand, Jimmy Reed played a Kay K-161 ThinTwin guitar, whose shield displayed a crown with three round circles representing jewels.

Furthermore, as noted by 'Niall' in his blog, Van Morrison wrote a song called "Perfect Fit," which in Rogan's opinion is "a *transparent* paean to [Morrison's girlfriend] Michelle Rocca." This song contains the line "see that *dress* you're wearing baby *suits you* right down to the ground," while Dylan's line 25 goes: "*transparent* woman in a *transparent dress*, it *suits you* well I must confess." This paraphrase is more doubtful though.

One more thing that strengthens that idea is that Bob Dylan seldom used the word *mystic,* found in only four songs, counting this one (line 10), while Van Morrison used it often in his songs, so much so this word is often associated with his name, one more bit of evidence Dylan alludes to Van Morrison in this song.

Line 8, "Go Tell It on the Mountain" is an Afro-American spiritual, but it was borrowed by James Baldwin for his novel, published in 1953, that focuses on the role of the Pentecostal Church in the lives of African Americans, and how it is a source of guilt for them. These associations are timely for a song about a bluesman, and about Van Morrison, who alluded to the Pentecostalism in some of his songs.

19	They threw everything at me, everything in the book
20	I had nothing to fight with but a butcher's hook
21	They had no pity, they never lent a hand
22	I can't sing a song that I don't understand
23	Goodbye Jimmy Reed, goodbye and good luck
24	I can't play the record 'cos my needle got stuck

The third and fourth verses could describe the early career of Bob Dylan, and the criticism he received from fans and the press. Van Morrison as well had his ups and downs. Much like Dylan, he went from one kind of music to another, not caring about his fans' demands.

Line 20, the "butcher's hook" alludes to Jimmy Reed's work in a meat plant to make a living, and next line to the hard times blues musicians met with when they asked to get paid for studio sessions and concerts.

Line 22 could mean Jimmy Reed's alcoholism hastened his decline and he needed his wife on stage to whisper his own lyrics to him. Line 24 could mean Jimmy Reed is plowing the same furrow, or else that writing songs became harder and harder, but we cannot help seeing some sexual allusion.

25	Transparent woman in a transparent dress
26	Suits you well I must confess
27	I break open your grapes, I'll suck out the juice
28	I need you like my head needs a noose
29	Goodbye Jimmy Reed, goodbye and so long
30	I thought I could resist her, but I was so wrong

The fifth verse could allude to Michelle Rocca, as said above, or else it could be linked to Jimmy Reed's alcoholism, the "transparent dress" and the *juice* of *grapes* make us think of wine, and alcohol addiction is like a *noose* around the *head*.

31	God be with you, brother dear
32	If you don't mind me asking, what brings you here
33	Ah nothing much, I'm just looking for the man
34	Came to see where he's lying in this lost land
35	Goodbye Jimmy Reed, and everything within you
36	Can't you hear me calling from down in Virginia

Dylan may be talking to Morrison when he says "God be with you, brother dear." But it recalls as well a Country song, "That's the Man I'm Looking For," that itself refers to Pontius Pilate pointing to the Christ saying "Ecce homo," that is the man. Plus, lines 31-32 are borrowed from Act 2, Scene 2 of a theatre play written in 1672 by the French playwright and actor Molière, *Les Femmes savantes* (*The Learned Ladies*).

Line 33, the narrator "is looking for the man," as *Van the Man* is Morrison's most frequent nickname, sometimes used by himself at his shows.

Once more, a Bob Dylan song is not what it seemed at first sight. What is claimed as a tribute to Jimmy Reed is just as well a tribute to Van Morrison. We may think Dylan began to write a tribute to Jimmy Reed and that his inspiration drifted, and as he read Van Morrison's biography by Johnny Rogan a while before, he mixed these two popular music figures, for he likes them both and he knows the former, Jimmy Reed, was a great influence on the latter, Van Morrison. There is a possibility Dylan and Morrison had a conversation about Jimmy Reed and talked of the place "where he's lying in this lost land" – Reed was buried in 1976 in a Chicago suburb.

Van Morrison began his career around the same time as Bob Dylan, first as a singer in groups like The Monarchs and Them. His first solo album, *Astral Weeks*, is still considered as one of the best in the second half of the twentieth century. His most famous song is "Gloria." He still sings it live sometimes, and the audiences join in on its chorus – "G.L.O.R.I.A." "Gloria" was covered by dozens of artists, particularly The Doors and Patti Smith. Bob Dylan and Van Morrison toured together in the U.S. and in Europe in 1998. They played together before: in 1976, Van Morrison sang at *The Last Waltz* show, and duetted with Dylan on "I Shall Be Released;" in the 1980s and 1990s, Van sang a track or two at several of Dylan's shows; in June 1989, both sang five of Van's songs on Mouson

Hill, the Hill of Muses, opposite to Athens Acropolis, for a documentary film by the BBC.

Van covered Dylan's "It's All Over Now Baby Blue" and "Just Like a Woman"; in 1982, live in Essen, Germany, he quoted a line from Dylan's song, "Idiot Wind," in his own song "Summertime in England;" in 1986, Van wrote a song for Bob, "Foreign Window." And Bob covered at least two of Van's songs live: "Carrying a Torch" and "Tupelo Honey." They both covered the same songs by other artists: "It's All in the Game," "Frankie and Johnny," "Wild Mountain Thyme," "You Don't Know Me;" and they wrote a song with the same name, but different lyrics on a similar topic, called "In the Garden."

Actually, Dylan would rather not dedicate a song to a living person directly. So, he used a tricky ploy to honor and brotherly salute two musicians he esteems. At the same time, he recognizes the music played by Jimmy Reed, the blues, knowing it is out of fashion, but it still has the power to change sadness into a celebration of hope and life.

9 - Mother of Muses

Who was the mother of Muses? The Muses are the daughters of Mnemosyne, Titan goddess of memory, and of Zeus, king of the gods. There are nine Muses: Calliope, Clio, Erato, Euterpe, Melpomene, Polyhymnia, Terpsichore, Thalia, and Urania. Diodorus of Sicily stated that Osiris first recruited the nine Muses, while passing through Ethiopia, before embarking on a tour of all Asia and Europe, teaching the arts of cultivation wherever he went. Hesiod narrates that the Muses brought forgetfulness to people. Apollo, the god of music, dance and poetry, of truth and prophecy, was their leader.

Calliope, whom Dylan is "falling in love with," is the Muse of eloquence and epic poetry. Hesiod and Ovid called her the "Chief of all Muses." She had two children with Apollo, one was Orpheus, already mentioned in the chapter on "False Prophet." She was sometimes believed to be Homer's muse for the Iliad and the Odyssey.

1	Mother of muses sing for me
2	Sing of the mountains and the deep dark sea
3	Sing of the lakes and the nymphs of the forest
4	Sing your hearts out all ye women of the chorus
5	Sing of honor and faith and glory be
6	Mother of muses sing for me
7	Mother of muses sing for my heart
8	Sing of a love too soon to depart
9	Sing of the heroes who stood alone

10	Whose names are engraved on tablets of stone
11	Who struggled with pain so the world could go free
12	Mother of muses sing for me

Plato and Neoplatonism made the Muses the mediators between the god and the poet or any intellectual creator, according to the conception of art which says the poet is possessed, put in a trance by the god, or else by his art. Homer involved the Muses in the Odyssey, and Virgil in the Aeneid. Ovid, Dante, Shakespeare, and Milton invoked them in their works. Dylan is familiar with these authors, he is especially attracted, maybe fascinated by ancient Greek and Roman culture. In New Orleans, the Muses each have a street to their name, and Dylan likes this city, since he owns a house there. He recorded the album *Oh Mercy* in this city in 1989.

At the private reception for the delivery of the Nobel prize medal to Bob Dylan, the Secretary of the Academy, Sara Danius, reported that Dylan looked for a long time at the medal's reverse, that shows a young man sitting under a laurel listening to the Muse. The inscription around this drawing is drawn from Virgil's Aeneid: "Inventas vitam juvat excoluisse per artes," "those who enriched our lives with the newfound arts they forged." This medal most likely inspired Bob Dylan to write the song "Mother of Muses."

Line 2, the "deep dark sea" recalls Homer who told of a "wine-dark sea." Actually, the Greeks at the time (eighth century B.C.) did not see colors the same way as we do: they did not know as many hues and did not use as many names for them. Those terms were meant to evoke feelings or impressions, in this case the sea was threatening.

13	Sing of Sherman, Montgomery and Scott
14	And of Zhukov and Patton and the battles they fought
15	Who cleared the path for Presley to sing
16	Who carved the path for Martin Luther King
17	Who did what they did and they went on their way
18	Man, I could tell their stories all day

The third verse refers to key figures in the second World War, Frederick C. Sherman, Bernard Montgomery, Thomas Patrick Scott, George Zhukov and George S. Patton. It reminds us they worked for the next generations. They are the modern equivalents of the heroes of Antiquity: Achilles, Hector, Agamemnon.

19	I'm falling in love with Calliope
20	She don't belong to anyone, why not give her to me
21	She's speaking to me, speaking with her eyes
22	I've grown so tired of chasing lies
23	Mother of muses, wherever you are
24	I've already outlived my life by far
25	Mother of muses unleash your wrath
26	Things I can't see they're blocking my path
27	Show me your wisdom, tell me my fate
28	Put me upright, make me walk straight
29	Forge my identity from the inside out
30	You know what I'm talking about

Line 25, the "wrath" refers to the Iliad, that describes the wrath of Achilles and its consequences.

| 31 | Take me to the river, release your charms |
| 32 | Let me lay down once in your sweet lovin' arms |

33	Wake me, shake me, free me from sin
34	Make me invisible like the wind
35	Got a mind to ramble, got a mind to roam
36	I'm traveling light and I'm a-slow coming home

Line 31 quotes the song "Take Me to The River," recorded by the soul singer Al Green.

Line 33, "Wake Me, Shake Me" was a radio jingle, which can be found on the Library of Congress web site, from the year 1939. Then in 1960, Billy Guy, the leader of the Rythm'n'Blues group The Coasters, made a song out of it. This song was covered in 1966 by The Blues Project, a group that included Al Kooper, famous for his organ improvisation on the phrase which opens "Like a Rolling Stone."

"Free me from sin" is a religious reference, from the Epistle to the Romans, in the New Testament.

Line 35 is influenced by the blues, e.g. the song "Roaming and Rambling" by Tampa Red, a musician Dylan covered in the 1970s. Jimmie Rodgers used the word "ramble" too in his song "My Rough and Rowdy Ways."

Line 36 contains three Leonard Cohen titles from the three last albums he created before his death: "Traveling Light" from the album *You Want It Darker* (referenced in "Murder Most Foul"), "Going Home" from *Old Ideas*, and "Slow" from *Popular Problems*. Does Dylan suggest Cohen's soul passed in him and became a part of his own mind? Thanks to what Leonard left to him, Bob can "travel light" for he acquired new abilities of composing. "Slow coming home" can also refer to Ulysses, for his return home took him several years, as related by Homer in the Odyssey.

Cohen and Dylan met several times and held each other in high esteem. Dylan covered "Hallelujah," one of Cohen's best-known songs, live in 1988. When Dylan received the Nobel Prize for Literature, Cohen declared: "To me [the award] is like pinning a medal on Mount Everest for being the highest mountain." Dylan sang backing vocals on "Don't Go Home with Your Hard-on" on Cohen's 1977 album, *Death of a Ladies Man*.

Here's what Cohen said of Dylan, in the 1980s: "A lot of people want to write Bob Dylan off. I'm not one of them. Doesn't matter if Bob takes a 10-year rest. First of all, if Bob never sang again, he's got a catalogue of work that will ensure his reputation into the next millennium. But I don't think that's the case anyway. I think he is Picasso. I think he's resting, and one of these days you're going to hear from him again. Something's going to come up and you'll hear him talking about himself or the world again and it's gonna turn you around. I just know it's gonna be that way. The last time we met for any great length of time was after a concert he'd done in Paris. We met in a café in the 14th arrondissement and we had a real good writers' shop talk. We really went into the stuff very technically. You couldn't meet two people who work more differently. He said, 'I like this song you wrote called "Hallelujah".' In fact, he started doing it in concert. He said, 'How long did that take you to write?' And I said, 'Oh, the best part of two years'. He said, 'Two years?' Kinda shocked. And then we started talking about a song of his called "I and I" from *Infidels*. I said, 'How long did you take to write that?' He said, 'Ohh, 15 minutes.' I almost fell off my chair. Bob just laughed."

And what Dylan said about Cohen: "When people talk about Leonard, they fail to mention his melodies, which to me, along with his lyrics, are his greatest genius. Even the counterpoint lines – they give a celestial character and melodic lift to every one of his songs. As far as I know, no one else comes close to this in modern music. His gift or genius is in his connection to the music of the spheres."

Cohen and Dylan have sometimes been compared, but they have more differences than similarities. Cohen's lyrics are much more personal, less universal than Dylan's, and the way he sings cannot be compared to the way Dylan sings, even though he decided to sing after hearing Dylan's first albums. Dylan's voice, his tones and his phrasing, are much more varied than Cohen's, whether you like them or not. In an argument, they agreed to say that if Cohen was number one, then Dylan would be number zero.

After "I've Made Up My Mind to Give Myself to You," "Mother of Muses" is the second song influenced by the Great American Songbook, given the way that Dylan sings and the song's rhythm.

Invoking the Muses and reciting a list of heroes' names, Bob Dylan connects to ancient poets, to the tradition of Homer, Virgil, and others. Every chorus begins with a call to the mother of Muses, as Homer began the Odyssey: "Tell me, O Muse...", and the Iliad: "Sing, goddess..."

The "Mother of Muses" recalls one of most famous Dylan songs, "Mr. Tambourine Man," which was also a call to the muse, and had a soft and pleasant melody as well. But inspiration is harder to find, the "jingle-jangle rhymes" are far away, so the singer must declare his love to Calliope, hoping she gives him a little attention and inspires him still with a few poems. Likewise, Leonard Cohen's inspiration left him for long periods of time, but when the end of his life was drawing close, the muse agreed to reward him with a few beautiful songs.

10 - Crossing the Rubicon

"Crossing the Rubicon" takes us back to ancient Rome: everyone heard of this episode, when Julius Caesar crossed the river Rubicon, in 49 BC. Caesar was ordered by the Roman Senate to stay with his army on the North bank of the Rubicon, that formed the frontier between Italy, administered directly by Rome, and the Cisalpine Gaul, ruled by a governor, Julius Caesar himself. He did not follow it, and crossed the Rubicon, which implied a war declaration to the Roman Republic. A civil war ensued, that ended the Roman Republic, and established the Roman Empire. At this event, Caesar said the famous sentence *alea jacta est* (in Greek, not in Latin, according to modern historians) – *the die is cast*. It means that events have passed a point of no return.

Dylan starts each verse with a threatening voice, as in "False Prophet," but comes back to softness halfway through the verse, and sings each time the title words with a tone expressing the state of things, even a regret for having crossed the Rubicon. The melody is inspired by Little Walter's song "Can't Hold Out Much Longer," only slowed down.

1	I crossed the Rubicon on the 14th day of the most dangerous month of the year
2	At the worst time at the worst place - that's all I seem to hear
3	I got up early so I could greet the Goddess of the Dawn
4	I painted my wagon - I abandoned all hope and I crossed the Rubicon

Line 1, the real event of crossing the Rubicon by Caesar was on January 10, not 14. But April 14 evokes Ruination
Day, as Gillian Welch sang it in her album *Time (The Revelator)*. President Lincoln was assassinated on 14 April 1865, the
Titanic hit the iceberg on 14 April 1912, the Black Sunday Dust
Storm hit Oklahoma on 14 April 1935, as sung by Woody Guthrie. Furthermore, Julius Caesar was assassinated on the Ides of
March, that is just one day after, the 15th. It was the deadline
for Romans to settle debts, "I pawned my watch, I paid my
debts" (line 16) alludes to it. Dylan was a member of the Latin
Club in his school in Hibbing, and this "Societas Latina" cele-
brated the Ides of March each year, so there is no doubt he
knows this date and its meaning. He most probably thought
too of the tax deadline day in the U.S., that is April 15.

The song mentions several times the dawn, and its
goddess, and ends with a look to the East, which does not
respect historic truth, Caesar looked to the south when he
crossed the Rubicon. It may evoke the narrator's hope his day
will be rewarding.

Line 4, "paint my wagon" can mean to have something
to do absolutely before doing another thing – often after a
defeat. It may refer also to the western film *Paint Your Wagon*, adapted from the 1951 musical of the same name.

"I abandoned all hope" refers to the beginning of the
Inferno (Hell) by the Italian poet Dante: "Abandon all hope, ye
who enter here." Dylan already alluded to Dante in the song
"Tangled Up in Blue" in the album ***Blood on The Tracks***, "an
Italian poet from the thirteenth century."

5	The Rubicon is the Red River, going gently as she flows
6	Redder than your ruby lips and the blood that flows from the rose
7	Three miles north of purgatory - one step from the great beyond
8	I prayed to the cross and I kissed the girls and I crossed the Rubicon

Line 5, the Rubicon is indeed the Red River, so named for it carries red mud, *Rubicon* and *red* have the same Latin origin. In this case, the red color alludes to the blood, which Caesar's decision contributed to spread. There are several Red Rivers in the U.S., a Northern one ends in Canada, and a Southern one flows in Texas and Louisiana. Dylan's song "Red River Shore," released in 2008, most likely is about the Northern Red River, that flows into the Lake Winnipeg.

Line 7, "Three miles north of purgatory" is another double allusion to Dante's *Divine Comedy*, that is divided in three parts: *Inferno (Hell), Purgatorio (Purgatory), and Paradiso (Paradise)*.

9	What are these dark days I see in this world so badly bent
10	How can I redeem the time - the time so idly spent
11	How much longer can it last - how long can this go on
12	I embraced my love put down my head and I crossed the Rubicon
13	I feel the bones beneath my skin and they're tremblin' with rage
14	I'll make your wife a widow - you'll never see old age
15	Show me one good man in sight that the sun shines down upon
16	I pawned my watch and I paid my debts and I crossed the Rubicon

Line 9, "badly bent" is borrowed from the ironic song by Little Walter "Dead Presidents," that mentions William

McKinley, the president mentioned in the first line of "Key West."

Line 10, "redeem the time" recalls Shakespeare's Sonnet 100:

Return, forgetful muse, and straight redeem
In gentle numbers time so idly spent

and lines in the Bible – Ephesians 5:15-16:

See then that ye walk circumspectly,
not as fools, but as wise,
Redeeming the time,
because the days are evil

Dylan evokes again the themes of mortality and the remaining time, as in the previous songs. Time and its restraints are often evoked in this song's first half: the 14th day, I got up early, the Red River flows, redeem the time, how much longer, how long, you'll never see old age, I pawned my watch...

Line 16, "I pawned my watch" recalls Elizabeth Cotton's song, "Shake Sugaree," covered live by Dylan in 1997. Elizabeth Cotten was a left-handed guitarist and singer of blues and folk, who invented a fingerpicking technique which influenced numerous musicians. Her most well-known song "Freight Train" was covered by the Quarrymen, the first group including Paul McCartney and John Lennon, before The Beatles.

17	Put my heart upon the hill where some happiness I'll find
18	If I survive then let me love - let the hour be mine
19	Take the high road - take the low, take the one you're on
20	I poured the cup and I passed it along and I crossed the Rubicon

Line 19, "Take the high road, take the low," is a line in a Scottish traditional ballad, "The Bonnie Banks of Loch Lomond." The low road leads the dead-at-battle soldiers directly to Scotland. Dylan probably knows this song by Liam Clancy, or by Tommy Makem, who played with the Clancy Brothers. In the Scorsese documentary, *No Direction Home*, Dylan recognizes he was influenced by the Clancy Brothers. One of their standards, "The Parting Glass," inspired Dylan's song "Restless Farewell," and "The Patriot Game" which influenced "With God on Our Side." In *Chronicles*, he wrote they sang "rousing rebel songs" at the White Horse Tavern on Hudson Street in downtown New York. For Dylan's thirtieth anniversary at Columbia recording company, in 1992, he went after the Madison Square Gardens show to Tommy Makem's Irish Pavilion in Midtown Manhattan with friends George Harrison, Eric Clapton and others. There, they drank and sang all night.

Now in "Crossing the Rubicon," Dylan thinks of the high road, the right one, even though it is harder and not so popular, the one he often took in his career. Robert Allen Zimmerman can be said to having crossed the Rubicon many times. First he left Hibbing, his childhood town, for trying his luck under the name of Bob Dylan; then he gave up "protest songs" for more personal songs; he made an outrageous speech when he was invited to receive the Tom Paine Award, in 1964, as we already mentioned; he played with an electrified group in 1965; he released a Country album, **Nashville Skyline**, at a time when this kind of music was viewed as corny and square; in 1979-80, he sang religious songs only, and preached at his shows; and lastly he released three albums of American standards, while his voice was anything but a crooner's.

Again, as in "My Own Version of You," figures of Julius Caesar and Jesus Christ conflate: "I prayed to the cross," "I stood between Heaven and Earth," "I poured the cup, I passed it along." The latter refers to the Gospel according to Matthew (26:39): "O my Father, if it be possible, let this cup pass from me: nevertheless not as I will, but as thou wilt."

21	You defiled the most lovely flower in all of womanhood
22	Others can be tolerant - others can be good
23	I'll cut you up with a crooked knife and I'll miss you when you're gone
24	I stood between heaven and earth and I crossed the Rubicon
25	You won't find any happiness here - no happiness or joy
26	Go back to the gutter and try your luck - find you some nice young pretty boy
27	Tell me how many men I need and who I can count upon
28	I strapped my belt and buttoned my coat and I crossed the Rubicon
29	I feel the Holy Spirit inside and see the light that freedom gives
30	I believe it's within the reach of everyman who lives
31	Keep as far away as possible - it's darkest 'fore the dawn
32	I turned the key and I broke it off and I crossed the Rubicon

Line 29, Dylan puts together the Holy Spirit and the freedom, which refers to the Bible (2 Corinthians 3:17): "Now the Lord is that Spirit: and where the Spirit of the Lord is, there is liberty." The light brought by freedom is the light God gives to the ones he speaks to – Exodus 34:29, Moses' face shone while the Lord talked with him. It refers as well to Betty Mae Fikes, a singer and Civil Rights Movement activist, who inserted political messages into well-known traditional or spiritual songs. She added "I've got the light of freedom" to the song "This Little Light of Mine" (which was also sung by Ray Charles or Sister Rosetta Tharpe). She took part in non-violent demonstrations in the 1960s, and sang for the last time in July 2020 at the burial of John Lewis, former chairman of the Student Nonviolent Coordinating Committee.

Line 31, "darkest 'fore the dawn" was used before by Dylan in his 1974 song, "Meet Me in the Morning."

Likewise, line 32, the key that broke recalls "the doorknob broke" in "Desolation Row," the last song on the album **Highway 61 Revisited**. The verb break off can also mean 'terminate,' close to cross the Rubicon.

33	Mona Baby, are you still in my mind - I truly believe that you are
34	Couldn't be anybody else but you who's come with me this far
35	The killing frost is on the ground and the autumn leaves are gone
36	I lit the torch and I looked to the east and I crossed the Rubicon

Line 33, Dylan previously used the name Mona no less than four times in his songs "To Ramona," "Stuck Inside of Mobile," "Visions of Johanna," "I Wanna Be Your Lover." The most recent was written in 1966, then we understand why he wonders if she is still in his mind.

Line 35 may refer to the blues line "killing floor," and the autumn leaves gone may mean death is near.

Line 36, the narrator looked to the East – which inspired the whole album – before crossing the Rubicon, that is crossing the path to the after-world, where a lit torch might be useful.

Bob Dylan refers to the Antiquity, religious texts, and key figures, historically or personally, and transposes them to his present situation. He reflects on time and the human condition. "Crossing the Rubicon" may be a metaphor for leaving this world to another unknown world, without any hope of return.

11 - Key West (Philosopher Pirate)

For those who do not know, Key West is an island off the coast of Florida, the southernmost and westernmost point in the contiguous United States, only ninety nautical miles from Cuba. President Kennedy often recalled this closeness in his speeches when he talked of Cuba. The name 'Key West' derives from the Spanish Cayo Hueso, the Bone Caye (i.e. low island). It is said that the island was littered with the bones of prior native inhabitants, who used the isle as a communal graveyard. The total land area is of 4.2 square miles, and the maximum elevation is about eighteen feet. In 1982, it was declared as a micro-nation to the UNO, under the name of *Conch* Republic – a name originally for someone with Europe-an ancestry who immigrated from the Bahamas, now applied to all residents of Key West – but this name has been main-tained only as a tourism booster for the city. Many American presidents, writers, actors, artists stayed on the island, and adventurers and pirates before them.

The melody is soft, with the sound of a harmonium in the background, but its rhythm is marked by a guitar. Each line starts with a major chord, C or F, but ends with an A minor chord, that gives a melancholic tone and encourages us to keep listening, same as the silences at the end of the third verse, "on the horizon line," and at the end of the tenth verse, "the land of light."

1	McKinley hollered, McKinley squalled
2	Doctor said, "McKinley, death is on the wall"
3	Say it to me if you got something to confess
4	I heard all about it, he was goin' down slow
5	I heard it on the wireless radio
6	From down in the boondocks, way down in Key West

The first two lines are borrowed from the song "White House Blues," written by Charlie Poole, a banjoist, and leader of the North Carolina Ramblers from 1925 to 1930. Dylan mentioned him in his Nobel Prize speech and acknowledged another of his songs, "You Ain't Talkin' to Me," inspired him. Charlie Poole sang "White House Blues" in 1926, but Dylan knew this song by a late 1950s group, the New Lost City Ramblers. He listened a lot to them and used many of their lyrics in the album *"Love and Theft"*.

William McKinley was the president of the United States from 1897 to his assassination in 1901, at the time of the Spanish-American war. Cuba was governed by the Spanish, and wanted its independence. The military ship *USS Maine* was sent to ensure the Americans' safety in Cuba, but it exploded in Havana's harbor, and no one knew why. The American press picked up on the story, saying it was sunk by the Spanish, claiming it was an act of war. McKinley temporized and tried to negotiate an agreement with Spain for the independence of Cuba, but the public opinion pushed to war. He gave in for it was election year, and the U.S. and Spain went into war in 1898. After a very deadly war, the U.S. won and Cuba was under their supervision for a few years, until it became independent in 1902.

A parallel can be made between McKinley, who tried to avoid the war with Spain, and gave in because of the manipulation of public opinion, and was killed three years later, and J. F. Kennedy, who rejected an operation to invade Cuba, and was killed two years later. In 1962, Chiefs of General Staff proposed to the executive powers a plan to invade Cuba and chase Fidel Castro. The operation *Northwoods* called for CIA operatives to both stage and commit acts of violent terrorism against American military and civilian targets, blaming them on the Cuban government, and using it to justify a war against Cuba. Some claim that JFK's refusal of this operation, in addition to the Bay of Pigs invasion's failure – decided in April 1961 unbeknownst to the president – are not unrelated to his assassination. President Teddy Roosevelt, who came after McKinley, was much more in favor of war, likewise President Lyndon Johnson who came after JFK engaged considerably more in the Vietnam war, especially after the Gulf of Tonkin incident in August 1964, whose later investigation revealed that the second attack never happened and was made up by the NSA.

The term "going down slow" can be found in numerous blues, Howlin' Wolf's among others. McKinley "was going down slow," he survived the attack, but died eventually from gangrene, caused by his injuries. He had some time to say goodbye to his wife, and together they sang "Nearer My God to Thee," a nineteenth century Christian choral. This hymn was sung on the Titanic as she was sinking, which makes us think of the song "Tempest," and the 1980 song "Caribbean Wind" that mentions it. It refers to Jacob's dream in Genesis, where angels ascend and descend a stairway or ladder to heaven.

Line 5, the narrator mentions the radio, which will be a guiding thread all over this track. Line 6, the song "Down in the Boondocks" is cited in "Murder Most Foul" too.

7	I'm searching for love, for inspiration
8	On that pirate radio station
9	Coming out of Luxembourg and Budapest
10	Radio signal's clear as can be
11	I'm so deep in love that I can hardly see
12	Down in the flatlands, way down in Key West
13	Key West is the place to be
14	If you're looking for immortality
15	Stay on the road, follow the highway sign
16	Key West is fine and fair
17	If you lost your mind, you'll find it there
18	Key West is on the horizon line

Radio Luxembourg was the only radio station that broadcast pop music, at a time when English radio stations broadcast only mainstream music. It was a legal radio station but listening to it was supposed to be forbidden in England, so as not to compete with the BBC. If you listened to it, you were kind of a pirate. This radio station had a powerful transmitter and you could get it in Western Europe, especially in England. Dylan probably heard it when he stayed in London in the 1960s, maybe with his friend John Lennon. This may allude to this musician, who Dylan already mentioned in the album *Tempest*. At least one pirate radio station broadcast from Budapest, Tilos Radio. Van Morrison mentions Radio Luxembourg, and Budapest, in his song "In the Days Before Rock'N'Roll," in the 1990 album *Enlightenment*. In Key West, there is a radio station named *Pirate Radio Key West*. The singer Jimmy Buffet, a Key West usual resident, wrote a song titled "A Pirate Looks at Forty." Dylan covered it once in 1982, and most likely thought of it while writing his own song, "Key West (Philosopher Pirate)." Lastly, in *Chronicles* Dylan wrote lines about the song "Pirate Jenny," from Bertolt Brecht's Threepenny Opera. For him it was a "song that made the strongest impression."

Line 12, the "flatlands" recalls the song "Highlands," on the album *Time Out of Mind*. A parallelism could be set between this 1997 song and "Key West," as if the latter would surpass the former. "Highlands" main topic is looking for peace of mind through escaping the present situation in search of a higher one, while "Key West" topic seems to embody the blissful feeling one has when he/she recognizes that the present situation is the one where we can find "immortality" and "the horizon line."

19	I was born on the wrong side of the railroad track
20	Like Ginsberg, Corso and Kerouac
21	Like Louis, and Jimmy and Buddy and all the rest
22	Well, it might not be the thing to do
23	But I'm sticking with you through and through
24	Down in the flatlands, way down in Key West
25	I got both my feet planted square on the ground
26	Got my right hand high with the thumb down
27	Such is life, such is happiness
28	Hibiscus flowers they grow everywhere here
29	If you wear one put it behind your ear
30	Down on the bottom, way down in Key West

Line 19, Dylan mentions a term he used in *Chronicles*, "wrong side of the railroad track," that is a deprived area, talking of his mother's family. He evokes the Beat poets, his friends Allen Ginsberg, Gregory Corso, Lawrence Ferlinghetti, and Jack Kerouac whom he never met but read the books. Then he mentions the pioneers of Rock'n'Roll Louis Jordan, Jimmy Reed, and Buddy Holly. All these people were somehow pirates, for they ignored conventions and carved out their own paths. Dylan referred to Louis Jordan in "Murder Most Foul" too, through the song "Let the Good Times Roll." Jordan was nicknamed the King of the Jukebox, which fits well **Rough and Rowdy Ways**' front sleeve. Dylan seems to like his song titles, since he was inspired by them in at least three of his songs: "Is You Is or Is You Ain't My Baby," "Ain't That Just Like a Woman," and "Open the Door, Richard."

Line 23, "I'm Stickin' with You" was sung by Little Willie John in 1956, and Jimmy Bowen around the same time, and the New York group The Velvet Underground ten years later. Dylan probably knows all three songs, but he would rather recall the older ones, which he listened to when he was a teenager.

31	Key West is the place to go
32	Down by the Gulf of Mexico
33	Beyond the sea, beyond the shifting sands
34	Key West is the gateway key
35	To innocence and purity
36	Key West, Key West is the enchanted land
37	I've never lived in the land of Oz
38	Or wasted my time with an unworthy cause
39	It's hot down here and you can't be overdressed
40	Tiny blossoms on a toxic plant
41	They can make you dizzy, I'd like to help you, but I can't
42	Down in the flatlands, way down in Key West

Line 36, Dylan mentions the "enchanted land," that is the Land of Oz, referred to three more times in "Key West":

line 33, the "shifting sands" are a way to access it ("Shifting Sands" is also the title of at least one American song); line 40, the "toxic plant" is the one that makes Dorothy – the heroine of the 1939 film *The Wizard of Oz* – sleep; and line 76, "my pretty little miss" was what the Wicked Witch called Dorothy, in that same movie: "I'll get you, my pretty, and your little dog, too!" This line was used in the sixth film in the *A Nightmare on Elm Street* franchise, *Freddy's Dead: The Final Nightmare*, released in 1991, which recalls its mention in "Murder Most Foul."

The creator of the books on the Land of Oz, L. Frank Baum, lived at the same time as President McKinley. He had a peculiar childhood, since four of the siblings died from illness, and he met many injured or coming back from war people. He reacted by immersing himself in Grimm's Fairy Tales. Meanwhile Spiritualism was in fashion, and the people tried to communicate with the dead. The Baum family was adept of Theosophy, and believed in dialogue with the dead, especially the ones in the family. According to his biographer Rebecca Loncraine, L. Frank Baum had a feeling he lived in an indeterminate place, between life and death, that is similar to Key West, as Dylan is describing it. When he died, his last words to his wife were "Now we can cross the shifting sands," to which Dylan alluded.

"Tiny blossoms on a toxic plant" allude to the lilies of the valleys, whose flowers are pretty, but very toxic. This flower is cited in chapter 2 of the *Canticle of Canticles*: "I am the rose of Sharon, and the lily of the valleys." Dylan refers to the rose of Sharon in his song mentioned above, "Caribbean Wind." Legend has it that the tears of the Virgin Mary at the foot of the cross gave birth to the flowers of the lily of the valleys.

43	Well, the fishtail palms and the orchid trees
44	They can give you that bleeding heart disease
45	People tell me I ought to try a little tenderness
46	On Newton Street, Bayview Park
47	Walking in the shadow after dark
48	Down under, way down in Key West

The "fishtails palms" are a genus of palm trees caryota, that grows south of Florida. Line 49, the gumbo-limbo, also known as turpentine tree, grows in the Neotropical realm.

Line 44, the "bleeding heart disease" is the name of a fungal disease, like the one Bob Dylan suffered in 1997. But it also refers to the Sacred Heart of Jesus, a Catholic devotion, wherein the heart of Jesus is viewed as a symbol of God's boundless and passionate love for mankind. It is depicted as a flaming heart shining with divine light, pierced by the lance-wound, encircled by the crown of thorns, surmounted by a cross, and bleeding. The wounds and crown of thorns allude to the manner of Christ's passion, while the flames represent a furnace of ardent love. On the other hand, upon hearing of Confederate General Stonewall Jackson's death, Robert E. Lee said: "I'm bleeding at the heart." Later, in the 1960s, "bleeding heart" came into common use, as a political insult for liberals. After that, the phrase was fully ensconced in political short-hand and quickly claimed by liberals as a positive trait.

"Try a Little Tenderness" is a song released for the first time in 1932, well-known for its cover by the soul singer Otis Redding in 1966. Dylan saw Otis live at the Whisky a Go Go in

Los Angeles, where he offered to cover his yet unreleased song "Just Like a Woman." Unfortunately Otis died before he could record it.

49	I play gumbo limbo spirituals
50	I know all the Hindu rituals
51	People tell me that I'm truly blessed
52	Bougainvillea blooming in the summer and the spring
53	Winter here is an unknown thing
54	Down in the flatlands, way down in Key West

The narrator talks of Spirituals, then of "Hindu rituals," alluding again to Eastern religions. Dylan displays all events on the same level, without any regard for anachronisms. He starts with an assassination that took place in 1901, and hearing it on the radio, even though radio broadcasting began in 1920 only. Hinduism and Buddhism tell that the past and future are constructions of the mind, it is the main premise of this song, in Key West time is only an illusion.

55	Key West is under the sun
56	Under the radar, under the gun
57	You stay to the left and then you lean to the right
58	Feel the sunlight on your skin
59	And the healing virtues of the wind
60	Key West, Key West is the land of light

Line 56, the "gun" refers to the form drawn by the Florida coasts and the Key islands on a map, same as the "hand high with the thumb down" (line 26). Although these words may allude to the Roman custom of sentencing to death or pardoning gladiators who fought in the arenas.

61	Wherever I travel, wherever I roam
62	I'm not that far from the convent home
63	I do what I think is right, what I think is best
64	History Street off of Mallory Square
65	Truman had his White House there
66	East bound, west bound, way down in Key West

Line 62 refers to the convent of Mary Immaculate, on Truman Avenue. President Truman, who ruled the United States from 1945 to 1953, stayed frequently in Key West. His doctor recommended him to go there for rest, so he bought himself a house, nicknamed Truman's Little White House. Today this building is a museum, and is still used as an official residence on certain occasions.

67	Twelve years old they put me in a suit
68	Forced me to marry a prostitute
69	There were gold fringes on her wedding dress
70	That's my story but not where it ends
71	She's still cute and we're still friends
72	Down on the bottom, way down in Key West

The twelfth verse tells Dylan's own story when he was twelve, at his Bar Mitzvah. Dylan compares himself to prophet Hosea, who realized he married a prostitute. He already mentioned this episode of the Bible in *Chronicles*, when he wrote on the song "Disease of Conceit." The story told in the Book of Hosea describes the relation between God and the Chosen People: she was an unfaithful wife because she was devoted to the cult of idols, while God is the husband, ready to forgive her at the slightest sign of repentance. The "gold fringes" are an ornament of the Torah, Hebrew scroll of the first five books of the Bible. And lines 70-71 show how Dylan feels about his ancestors' religion: he was forced to adopt it when he was a child, moved away from it in the years 1979-81, then he went deeper into it thanks to his friend Louie Kemp, explored other religions and philosophies, and now he recognizes the qualities of his original religion and holds no grudge against it. The root of the name Hosea is the same as the ones of Joshua and Jesus. The Christians extended this analogy to Jesus and his wife, the Church, as shown in the Bible, e.g. Ephesians 5:25: "Husbands, love your wives, even as Christ also loved the church, and gave himself for it." Dylan most likely thought of the Christian analogy, for he has been admiring the character of Jesus for decades. In "False Prophet," Dylan is "nobody's bride": he is linked to no church and no religion.

This song alludes to other marriages, those of President McKinley, and of the author of the Wizard of Oz, and in the fourth verse the hibiscus flower that Tahitian women put behind their right or left ear, meaning they are available, or not. Would Dylan mean tranquility and happiness should be found in the marriage? The word "marry" should not be taken literally, especially when you read the next verse.

73	I play both sides against the middle
74	Trying to pick up that pirate radio signal
75	I heard the news, I heard your last request
76	Fly around, my pretty little miss
77	I don't love nobody, give me a kiss
78	Down on the bottom, way down in Key West

Line 73, Dylan says "play both sides against the middle," meaning he takes the best in every religion or philosophy, rejecting none. Line 77, he insists, "I don't love nobody," otherwise said I do not belong to any organization, be it political or religious. As soon as his 1991 tour, Dylan introduced his song "Gotta Serve Somebody" saying "This is an anti-religion song." He stated again this conviction when in 2019 he sang it at every show, with different lyrics, making another song. This song is no more about religion, now it says the human being cannot help to submit to something in life.

It confirms what he said in September 1997: "Here's the thing with me and the religious thing. This is the flat-out truth: I find the religiosity and philosophy in the music. I don't find it anywhere else. Songs like 'Let Me Rest on a Peaceful Mountain' or 'I Saw the Light' – that's my religion. I don't adhere to rabbis, preachers, evangelists, all of that. I've learned more from the songs than I've learned from any of this kind of entity. The songs are my lexicon. I believe the songs."

Line 75, "I heard the news" is the first line of a Beatles song, "A Day in the Life," one more reference to John Lennon, who wrote this line.

Dylan continues by citing several song titles.

"Fly Around My Pretty Little Miss" is a traditional song recorded for the first time in 1924, and covered by the New Lost City Ramblers. This group was founded by Mike Seeger (Pete Seeger's half-brother), John Cohen and Tom Paley, and played from 1958 to 1960. Their purpose was to revive old-time music, without sanitizing it. Most of the tunes came through the compilation made in 1952 by Harry Smith, the *Anthology of American Folk Music*. John Cohen befriended

158

Dylan in the early 1960s, he was among the first to photograph and film him, when Dylan was yet unknown. The *Anthology of American Folk Music* was originally a three-album set, made of songs from 1926 to 1933. It had an enormous influence on American music. Many forgotten musicians were discovered again thanks to it, and its authenticity greatly inspired the Folk Revival Movement. Bob Dylan covered several songs from it, although he first heard most of those songs by the New Lost City Ramblers, or by bluesmen who were still alive in the 1960s. The *Anthology* was reissued on CD, with the addition of a fourth volume.

"I Don't Love Nobody" was sung in 1958 by Elizabeth Cotten, who was already mentioned in "Crossing the Rubicon."

"Gimme a Little Kiss" was sung by Frank Sinatra in 1946, in a puckish style. But Dylan most likely borrowed the second part of line 77 from the first line of the song "A Kiss to Build a Dream On," sung in 1951 by Louis Armstrong, then by Tony Bennett among others: "Give me a kiss to build a dream on." Is he building a dream in Key West?

"Meet Me in the Bottom" is a blues recorded in 1936, that draws from another blues, "Hey Lawdy Mama," dating from 1934. Both those songs and their variants were covered by many blues and blues-rock musicians: Lightnin' Hopkins, Howlin' Wolf, Willie Dixon, Freddie King, Eric Clapton, and so on. Dylan cited this phrase, altering it slightly, "Meet me in the bottom, bring me my running shoes," in "Workingman's Blues" in the album **Modern Times**.

Line 77 makes us think again of Van Morrison: the song "Give Me a Kiss" in Van's album *His Band and the Street*

Choir. In his interview about **Rough and Rowdy Ways**, Dylan says his songs were written in a state of trance, and that is what Van Morrison said for a long time when he was asked how he composed his own songs.

79	Key West is the place to be
80	If you're looking for immortality
81	Key West is paradise divine
82	Key West is fine and fair
83	If you lost your mind, you'll find it there
84	Key West is on the horizon line

Here the narrator sings again a kind of chorus, just one line differs from the previous one (lines 13-18). The "paradise divine" refers to the Paradise in Dante's *Divine Comedy*, and to John Milton's *Paradise Lost*. The words "fine and fair" reminisce the saying of the witches in Shakespeare's play, Macbeth: "fair is foul and foul is fair."

Bob Dylan stayed several times in the island of Key West, he even has a stool with his name on it, in a bar, *Captain Tony's Saloon*, opened sixty years ago by an adventurer, Tony Tarracino. This man started by taking over his father's bootlegging business, then became a professional gambler, had ties with the New Jersey mafia, whose soldiers left him for dead, upon which he settled in Key West in 1948, as a shrimper and gunrunner – a pirate's life in short. In 1961, he opened a bar under his name, at another bar's location, *Sloppy Joe*, which Hemingway patronized in the 1930s. He sold it in 1989, but stayed as a local figure and was elected mayor of Key West. Writers Truman Capote and Tennessee Williams were among the customers in this bar. The new landlord recalls that Tarracino told him of Dylan, "a quiet guy, he used to come around." Bob Dylan probably liked a place where he could philosophize in the company of pirates, or at least in the memory of past pirates... Like the French writer and song composer Pierre Mac Orlan, in Bob Dylan there is a lot of the "passive adventurer," who lives adventures by proxy, avoiding the hard-luck stories.

"Key West (Philosopher Pirate)" is probably the main song in the album, after "Murder Most Foul," and it foreshadows this track, which follows in the order Bob Dylan chose, with the same themes of president's assassinations and conspiracies.

The place Dylan describes makes us think of "Desolation Row," a spot where we land and that separates the narrator from the outside world. But Desolation Row was a dreadful and ominous place, while Key West seems to be a "paradise divine," where all issues are solved, the "enchanted land," "the land of light," "the place to be If you're looking for immortality."

The West is symbolic in numerous religions and creeds. To some native Americans, it is the wisdom that understands the peculiarities in everything, the assimilation of all the experiences in life, the door we open after the death of the Ego, the place to grow old, the way to merge fully with the spiritual consciousness, lastly the gate that leads to reincarnation. In the *Sagrada Familia*, the monumental cathedral by architect Antoni Gaudi in Barcelona, Spain, the Western frontage is dedicated to the Christ suffering during his crucifixion. In Celtic religion, the West was the threshold between life and the next transformation of the soul, which was mysterious for they did not know what came after. For ancient Egyptians, the West was the door to the Kingdom of the Dead, but it was not the last state of the body. In Buddhism, the West represents the movement toward Buddha, or the illumination. In Jewish religion, the West is the direction we take to get closer to God.

The United States of America created the "Wild West" and its Legend, which is decried nowadays, but if we look at its positive side, it was the door to freedom and adventure, the land of the pioneers. In the novel *The Great Gatsby*, F. Scott Fitzgerald, a writer Dylan refers to in at least three of his songs – "Ballad of a Thin Man," "When I Paint My Masterpiece," "Summer Days" – the West is a symbol of goodness. More recently, Jim Morrison sang it with The Doors in the song "The End" – "The West is the best."

The poet Wallace Stevens also made frequent visits to the island of Key West between 1922 and 1940, and wrote a poem titled "The Idea of Order at Key West." In a 1968 interview, Dylan called him a "great poet." Stevens evoked Florida in several poems, and one among the last, "Of Mere Being," refers to this uncertain state in life, when it is nearing its end. Key West is the key that allows to open a door by which we can reach an unknown land, a pleasant life forever, a state of conscience that seems like the sleep according to the Ancient Egyptians, a liminal state, like the Elysian Fields of the Ancient Greeks, or the dream of Jacob. But Bob Dylan, in his role of a "philosopher pirate," does not adopt any creed, and takes from all at his discretion, that is why he would rather not define this place precisely, leaving it to his listener's imagination.

12 - Shadow Kingdom

Shadow Kingdom is the name Bob Dylan gave to a new experience for him: a whole show filmed and broadcast in streaming. Viewing of this show was proposed during a limited period (from 18 to 20 July 2021, prolonged until 26 July) on the streaming platform Veeps, for the modest sum of 25 dollars, on sale from 16 June. The show was announced with a thirty-second video of the song "Watching the River Flow," in black and white pictures, with masked musicians. The comment mentioned "The Early Songs of Bob Dylan," while we would rather expect songs from the album *Rough and Rowdy Ways*, not yet played live. A press release said nothing more precise than "it will showcase the artist in an intimate setting as he presents renditions of songs from his extensive and renowned body of work created especially for this event." They reminded us it was "the artist's first concert performance since December 2019," and its "first broadcast performance in nearly 30 years," which was the *MTV Unplugged* 1994 show.

The meaning of this name, *Shadow Kingdom,* is somewhat of a mystery. It recalls the picture accompanying the song "False Prophet," inspired by an issue of the pulp magazine *The Shadow*. *The Shadow Kingdom* is also a short novel written by Robert E. Howard, released in 1929 in the magazine *Weird Tales*. This writer is well-known for his Heroic

Fantasy character *Conan the Barbarian*, whose adventures were offered as books, comic strips, film, and games. Robert E. Howard's novel may have inspired Bob Dylan. It presents us with "Serpent Men" who rule a Shadow Kingdom, and Howard found this theory in Helena Blavastky's writings. Now Dylan in the *Chronicles* borrowed from Blavastky's most famous book, *Isis Unveiled: A Master-Key to the Mysteries of Ancient and Modern Science and Theology*, written in 1877. Blavastky and the theosophic theories came into fashion again in the 1960s. Dylan most likely got interested in them at the time, and maybe he recalled the Howard stories he read when he was younger. In the song "Key West," Dylan alludes to the land of Oz, whose creator adhered to those theories. Isis is the name of a Dylan song, on the album *Desire*. Furthermore, Blavastky borrowed from many other writers for writing her books, which in all likelihood amused Bob Dylan.

Whatever, Bob Dylan's **Shadow Kingdom** is only vaguely related to Robert E. Howard's *The Shadow Kingdom*, as we shall see below. The "shadow" may also allude to the well-known "valley of the shadow of death" from the Bible, Psalm 23. The word used here for the shadow of death is *tsalmaveth* which actually means death-like shadow or deep shadow. So maybe Dylan was thinking of the "kingdom of death" when he named his show "Shadow Kingdom." The word *shadow* can be found too in the first album of covers of the Great American Songbook, **Shadows in the Night**, and this album's sleeve evokes the same atmosphere as the streaming show.

For Bob Dylan followers, the broadcasting of this show was the second big surprise in the years 2020, after the release of the album **Rough and Rowdy Ways**. It is actually a film directed by the filmmaker Alma Har'el, helped by Lol Crawley as Director of Photography. Dylan knew Har'el, for she used three of his songs – "Moonshiner," "Tomorrow is a Long Time," and "Series of Dreams" – in a 2011 documentary film, *Bombay Beach*. Critics noticed Har'el had the ability to artistically blur the lines between documentary and fiction, and this film was a "fever dream about an alternate universe." In *Shadow Kingdom*, everything was well thought out, the musicians' position and the way they play, the audience's moves, and the scenery in which they perform. Better still, musicians[1] did not play the music we can hear, they only mimed while a recorded music plays, and Dylan's voice too was recorded, as revealed by the absence of synchronization between sound and picture. Or else he sang during the filming and another recording of his voice was broadcast. The whole movie is in black and white, and Dylan's clothes are in the same colors. He left out his western boots to wear two-tone loafers, and wears a white or a black jacket, depending on each track. He sings center stage, unmasked, while all musicians wear a mask, and he plays the harmonica. He sometimes wears a guitar around his neck but does not seem to play it. Members of the audience (all actors) sit at tables or move through the room, some of them are dancing. They drink alcohol and smoke cigarettes, although some say it is artificial smoke, since the cigarettes do not seem to be consumed.

The end credits say the show happened at the "Bon Bon Club" in Marseilles, France, but this place never existed. It

---

[1] Bob Dylan played occasionally guitar and harmonica, accompanied by Buck Meek (guitar), Alexander Burke (accordion), Janie Cowan (bass), Joshua Crumbly (bass), Shahzad Ismaily (guitar, bass, banjo, accordion).

was shot in Santa Monica, California, in May 2021. The five musicians are unknown to the general public. They come from various musical backgrounds and their age is half Dylan's, even less. Accordion can be heard on every track, upright bass too, but no drums. At the real recording sessions, Dylan called in Don Was on bass, with whom he already played in 1990, on the album **Under the Red Sky**, and other less renowned musicians[2] on guitar, dobro, mandolin, and accordion.

We learned later the **Shadow Kingdom** sessions followed a three-day session in March 2021 to re-record six Bob Dylan songs. T-Bone Burnett, who toured with Dylan in 1975-76 on the Rolling Thunder Revue, invented a new medium to archive audio recordings, the *Ionic* disc, that features a coating that protects it from wear but can still be played on a typical record player. He convinced Dylan to record some of his old songs on this new format. They recorded "Blowin' in the Wind," "Gotta Serve Somebody," "Masters of War," "Simple Twist of Fate," "The Times They are A-Changin'," and "Not Dark Yet." They decided to sell them one at a time, one song on one side of a 10-inch acetate. The unique ionic disc of "Blowin' in the Wind" was auctioned in July 2022 where it sold for $1,769,508. Burnett said this sale was "a full rebellion against mass consumerism." He added these Ionic original discs are handmade, they cannot be mass produced for they are expensive and time consuming to make. Anyway, right after that short session, Dylan wanted to carry on and make a video. Recording it took a further three more months, and the result was **Shadow Kingdom**.

---

[2] Greg Leisz (guitar, dobro, mandolin and pedal steel guitar), Tim Pierce (guitar), Jeff Taylor (accordion).

The show consists of thirteen songs, nine from the 1960s, three from the 1970s – "When I Paint My Masterpiece" and "Watching the River Flow," to be heard again at the fall of 2021, plus "Forever Young" – and one from 1989 – "What Was It You Wanted," maybe as an answer to forthcoming critics. All the tracks are sung with a quite slow rhythm, "Most Likely You Go Your Way" and "Watching the River Flow" being the swiftest. Some are more talked than sung – "Tombstone Blues." During "I'll Be Your Baby Tonight," Dylan is between two young ladies, a white one and a black one, both looking at the audience. It provokes a feeling of uneasiness and goes against the cliches of the women staring at the masculine star. The songs are played nearly without interruption, and the musical transitions between them are much refined, which is very unusual for someone like Dylan who practiced musical genres as simple as Folk and Rock. The show lasts only fifty minutes, because this way the artist is certain to retain the attention of his audience, and that it receives well his message.

The arrangements for those old songs were completely modified. Dylan picked up what were sketches for him when recording them for the first time in the studio, and gave them "an appropriated structure," as he said in a 2004 interview. Doing this, he adapted them to his present artistic statute. As he reminded us in his Nobel speech, Shakespeare's plays were not definitely written at their first show, their text and their staging changed each time they were played, and still change nowadays. Like those theatre plays, Bob Dylan's songs are made for evolving in the future, after they were recorded. At the same time, they are strongly linked to the past, for their roots draw from the blues and all kinds of music and lyrics from the 1950s and before. Bob Dylan stated in a 1989 interview with Edna Gundersen: "Everybody works in the shadow of what they've previously done. But you have to overcome that." Thanks to his songs' re-actualization in this show and in the following tour, as seen further on, Dylan manages to link them at once to the past, the present, and the future – as he sang in "I Contain Multitudes," "Today and tomorrow, and yesterday."

The mood of the show resembles to that of a film noir, a genre Dylan likes a lot, but there is no plot. The checkered ground and the curtain recall the "Red Room" in the series *Twin Peaks*. In the background at the beginning of the show, behind Dylan, we catch sight of a boat model, a three-masted schooner, as we can imagine for pirates sailing the seas. On the last song, the set right next to Dylan looks like a sail. Are these allusions to the song "Key West (Philosopher Pirate)"? Everything in this show contributes to create an unreal impression, a dream feeling. Director Alma Har'el explained in an interview her aim is to create a dreamlike mood in her films. We have the premonition all is not revealed, that it is only a "shadow" show. Laura Tenschert on her web site *DefinitelyDylan* suggested **Shadow Kingdom** would be inspired by Shakespeare's play, *A Midsummer Night's Dream*. This comedy is kind of a dream, his characters dream all the time, the main character Puck sums it up at the last scene, speaking to the audience:

> If we shadows have offended,
> Think but this, and all is mended:
> That you have but slumbered here,
> While these visions did appear;
> And this weak and idle theme,
> No more yielding but a dream.

We may guess that, same as *A Midsummer Night's Dream* is the dream of a Shakespeare theater play, **Shadow Kingdom** is the dream of a Bob Dylan show.

Afterword

Rough and Rowdy Ways has no catchy melody, no riff as in "Like a Rolling Stone," no chorus as in "Blowin' in the Wind." Yet the mix is excellent, we can hear distinctly and perfectly each music instrument, even though they are played in a light and soft, nearly subliminal, way. Bob Dylan's voice is up front and very clear, his enunciation and his phrasing are excellent, and the drums and percussion are discreet but efficient. It is an album that creeps into your mind, that does not need to show its strength, the opposite of a "rowdy" album.

This album refers to all kinds of religions, myths, and philosophies: the Christian Old and New testaments, Judaism, Buddhism, Taoism, Ancient Egypt religion, Greek mythology, Heraclitus, … Could it be the religious album Dylan spoke about in 2012, at the release of the album ***Tempest***: "I wanted to make something more religious."

The album's music is rather soft, and its lyrics are sometimes "rough" but never "rowdy", so the "Rough and Rowdy Ways" are not the album's ways, instead they are the ways of our present world, which worsened since the 1960s, especially since in the Western world the people's trust in their leaders faded away, following several events, particularly a key event that happened when Bob Dylan was in his early twenties, at the end of his age of innocence, that is the assassination of President Kennedy. Fortunately, the arts and great thinkers' works help us to step back and continue to live in this world, a "foul" world in some ways.

Once more, Bob Dylan managed to surprise us and reinvent himself, by releasing an album that resembled no other, by its highest standards and its fine execution.

A feature common to all the songs is their epic breath. Also present are the moral values – wisdom, justice, truth, moderation, courage – that spread out, right next to their contraries. The album is a work of great unity, the same themes can be found in all its songs: political leaders' assassinations, conspiracies and plots, racism and civil wars, growing old and immortality, tributes to the artistic works, be they classical or popular: cinema, literature, poetry, novels, noir and gothic particularly, and music above all, with obvious or oblique references to the artists Dylan likes or acknowledges. As such, it is a meditation on America through its culture.

A reference to the same writing or writer can be found in several songs in the album, creating interactions between them. The songs are not the same, but they take up the same themes, Dylan meant just that in his June 2020 interview: "The individual pieces are just part of a whole." If you read the lyrics of a song keeping its references in mind, and you go onto another song, then go back to the first one, you will discover in the former ideas the latter evoked. The songs in this album make a cycle, which compares to Dante's works, even though Dylan most likely did not know that. As explained by Didier Ottaviani, who wrote a Philosophy PhD thesis about Dante, "once you got to the end, you must start again because at this time you may find in the first work something that the last work taught us. All is cyclic in Dante. It is a kind of eternal re-turn, but not of the same."

Rough and Rowdy Ways is also a *unique* work in Bob Dylan's career, in that he never wrote this way before. There were never as many references in one single album. You can find references to other works or people in all Bob Dylan's albums, but not in such a great number. Especially in "Murder Most Foul," nearly all lines contain at least one reference, often more. It is not plagiarism, since those references are in brief, and most of them are open, it is some kind of tribute. Dylan in his latest interview claims he is in a sort of trance when composing and that the songs came to him all made. But he may be answering that for any number of reasons. It may be partly true, but it is not really convincing, besides it is a way of avoiding blame and criticism by denying responsibility. As far as we know, he most likely used at least two methods to seek inspiration.

Dylan used before the cut-up method, he mentioned it in a 1995 interview. It is an aleatory literary technique in which a written text is cut up and rearranged to create a new text. The concept can be traced to at least the Dadaists of the 1920s but was popularized in the late 1950s and early 1960s by writer William S. Burroughs. Dylan is renowned for his habit of writing everything that interests him on pieces of paper, as he described in several interviews. He probably used this cut-up technique: he puts all those pieces of paper in a box, adds fragments of texts written by others and mixes them all, then draws one piece at a time from the box and makes a line or several lines out of them. Actually, the *cento* is a much older technique, it consists of taking verses or passages from other literary or musical works and arranging them in a new form or order. It has been much practiced in the 3rd or 4th century A.D., with the works of Homer and Virgil. It is not impossible Dylan knew of this literary technique. Some of his songs made us suspect it, for example, when he borrowed full passages from Junichi Saga or Henry Timrod in his albums *"Love and Theft"* and **Modern Times**.

Another method is thought associations, and sometimes Bob Dylan's thoughts seemed to take twisted paths, as illustrated before in this essay. Previously, references were most of the time direct, Dylan cited his takes word for word or modified them slightly. Now in this album references are often oblique, a word or a line evokes another word or sentence that are part of the same work or written by the same author. This type of inspiration can indeed happen in a state of mind likened to a trance. The writer is in a daze where all kinds of thoughts come to him, and he retains lines he arranges them in order to write a song. We can imagine it from Bob Dylan's numerous interviews (and Van Morrison's too), when he is asked about his songwriting. He tried and explained it in a 1991 interview with Paul Zollo: "It's nice to be able to put yourself in an environment where you can completely accept all the unconscious stuff that comes to you from the inner workings of your mind. And block yourself off to where you can control it all, take it down... [...] You ought to be able to sort out those [good and evil] thoughts, because they don't mean anything, they're just pulling you around, too. It's important to get rid of all them [evil] thoughts. Then you can do something from some kind of surveillance of the situation. You have some kind of place where you can see it but it can't affect you. Where you can bring something to the matter, besides just take, take, take, take." And again, in 2003 with Robert Hillburn: "What happens is, I'll take a song I know and simply start playing it in my head. I meditate on a song. I'll be playing [a song] in my head constantly – while I'm driving a car or talking to a person or sitting around or whatever. People will think they are talking to me and I'm talking back, but I'm not. I'm listening to the song in my head. At a certain point, some of the words will change and I'll start writing a song."

These distinctive features of Bob Dylan's songwriting since 1997 – the album *Time Out of Mind* – and even more since 2001 – *"Love and Theft"* – share many things with post-modern music. The sixteen characteristics of this kind of music, as they were defined by the composer and music theorist Jonathan Kramer[3], can be found mostly in Bob Dylan's music:

1. It "is not simply a repudiation of modernism or its continuation, but has aspects of both a break and an extension." Isn't that the reason why he received the Nobel prize, "for having created new poetic expressions within the great American song tradition?" From the 1960s on, Dylan has been known for relying on existing music to write his own, but at the same time he broke a few rules, as writing poetic lyrics in Rock'n'Roll music. He also extended some, as he was the first one to write a hit over three minutes, "Like a Rolling Stone," or writing songs that talked of love like never before.

2. It "is, on some level and in some way, ironic." Let us think of "Rainy Day Women #12 & 35" as ironic music, and about ironic lyrics, there is an embarrassment of riches! One of his first songs, "Talkin' John Birch Paranoid Blues" comes to mind, and

---

[3] Characteristics taken from Wikipedia article on Postmodern music.

there are many other examples, e.g., "False Prophet."

3. It "does not respect boundaries between sonorities and procedures of the past and of the present." Bob Dylan's music draws from all kinds of music and poetry from the twentieth century, and older ones too. His music is influenced by melodies from the 1920s to the present days, and his lyrics mix in the same song lines from the Antiquity (Homer), Dante, nineteenth century poets (Timrod, Poe), more recent writers (Ginsberg, Burroughs), and many others.

4. It "challenges barriers between 'high' and 'low' styles." In the same song, Dylan may address topics from everyday life, and higher topics, like religion, or the hardness of life, or racism. He may be inspired by a Salvation Army fanfare, or by some of the greatest poets.

5. It "shows disdain for the often unquestioned value of structural unity." Dylan is well-known for changing very often the structure of many of his songs. Yet it can be argued his songs have a musical structural unity, even though it changes. So, this feature is not 100% true.

6. It "questions the mutual exclusivity of elitist and populist values." Dylan does not care if his music and lyrics draw from classical or popular values, he mixes them all and treats them on an equal basis.

7. It "avoids totalizing forms (e.g., does not want entire pieces to be cast in a prescribed formal mold)." Same as before, a Bob Dylan song never

has a finished form, it is only a sketch that can be changed anytime.

8. It "considers music not as autonomous but as relevant to cultural, social, and political contexts." Well, if we review all of Dylan's songs, some of them were not really relevant to any context. *Another Side of Bob Dylan* wanted to break from "protest," but some of his songs, like "Chimes of Freedom," are still relevant to the social context. The album *Nashville Skyline* is probably the most irrelevant to social and political contexts, though it can be said its songs have a cultural context, since they were an incursion into Country music. *Pat Garrett and Billy The Kid* is peculiar since it was a film soundtrack, yet its well-known song "Knockin' on Heaven's Door" can be seen as having social and political contexts, since it tells the story of an outlaw who was killed by the progress of civilization. *Slow Train* and *Saved* contain songs that are relevant mostly to religion, and it may be taken as a cultural context, but *Shot of Love* contains at least one song with social and political contexts, "Lenny Bruce." Among the albums that were made partially or totally made of covers from other artists[4], one can argue the songs in the album *World Gone Wrong* were totally relevant to all three contexts, while the Christmas album and the three albums of songs from the Great American Songbook were definitely not relevant. Neverthe-

---

[4] Bob Dylan, Self Portrait, Knocked Out Loaded, Down in the Groove, Good as I Been to You, World Gone Wrong, Christmas in the Heart, Shadows in the Night, Fallen Angels, Triplicate.

less, most of the songs in Dylan's albums were relevant to cultural, social, and political contexts. It is obvious at the beginning of his career, with *The Freewheelin' Bob Dylan* and *The Times They Are A-Changin'*, and a bit less obvious in *Bringing It All Back Home* and *Highway 61 Revisited*. But even in the albums *Planet Waves* or *Street Legal*, you can find lines relevant to politics or at least social concerns, and the cultural context is never far away. The albums from 2001 on – *"Love and Theft"*, *Modern Times*, *Tempest* – allude to social and political issues, only they do not do it openly. In *Rough and Rowdy Ways,* it is more obvious, especially in "Murder Most Foul."

9.   It "includes quotations of or references to music of many traditions and cultures." As we have seen before in this essay, and as it has been developed in many other books on Bob Dylan, he just cannot write a song without quoting or referencing many traditions and cultures, in the lyrics and often in the music too. And his references go from the Greek and Roman Antiquity unto traditional songs from the eighteenth century – Robert Burns – and before, unto nineteenth century poets – Timrod, Shelley – unto twentieth century writers and musicians, in fact they are limitless.

10.   It "considers technology not only as a way to preserve and transmit music but also as deeply implicated in the production and essence of music." Dylan remains committed to a traditional technology for recording his songs. He went from analogue to digital with reluctance, and he still rec-

ords "live" in the studio, avoiding re-recording most of the time. On stage, he still uses microphones connected to wires. He submitted to technology once, in the album **Empire Burlesque**, and never tried again. So, technology is indeed for him "deeply implicated in the essence of music," as long as he chooses it and is not overwhelmed by it.

11. It "embraces contradictions." This characteristic could not be truer as it is the theme of "I Contain Multitudes," and one of the key themes in **Rough and Rowdy Ways**.

12. It "distrusts binary oppositions." It shows as early as 1964 in the song "My Back Pages," the line "Lies that life is black and white." Except for 1979-80, Dylan almost always expressed finely shaded opinions in his songs and interviews. As Joan Baez sang in "Diamonds and Rust," he was a master "at keeping things vague."

13. It "includes fragmentations and discontinuities." Many of Dylan's songs contain musical phrases and/or lines that seem to be out of place with the rest of the song. He is renowned to scatter his songs with metaphors that create an overall meaning, even though the lines do not seem to create a logical story.

14. It "encompasses pluralism and eclecticism." Dylan wrote and played all kinds of songs, from folk to blues to rock to reggae to gospel to pop to standards, you name it. "Subterranean Homesick Blues" has been called the first rap. His radio show, on

XM radio channel for two years, revealed his eclecticism.

15. It "presents multiple meanings and multiple temporalities." Dylan often said he tried to write lines with double or triple meaning. He also said time is not important in his songs, he may write a line at the present time, and the next one at a past or future time. In his film *Renaldo and Clara*, he claimed he wanted to stop time, and the song "Tangled Up in Blue," written at the same period, mixes the times to that same effect, to abolish the boundaries between past, present and future. The song "I Contain Multitudes" alludes to it in its first line, "Today and tomorrow, and yesterday."

16. It "locates meaning and even structure in listeners, more than in scores, performances, or composers." Bob Dylan sometimes asked his listeners to do their share when they listened to one of his records or shows, or when they watched one of his films. It was especially true when he released the film *Renaldo and Clara*, and the critics just did not care about the explanations he gave in lengthy interviews, they just reduced it to a three-person love affair between him, Sara, and Joan Baez. Every Bob Dylan album is different, so he expects you not to judge it by comparing to its previous album. Same for his shows, Dylan seldom played his songs the way they were recorded in the studio, and often played different versions of a song, so that the listener has to adapt him/herself to those new versions. Since 2021, in the **Rough and Rowdy Ways** tour, when you go to a Dylan show, you are

asked not to expect any big hit and really listen to what you are hearing. Dylan said it again in his just released book, *The Philosophy of Modern Song*, "Knowing a singer's life story doesn't particularly help your understanding of a song, it's what a song makes you feel about your own life that's important."

The professor of literature and musicology Daniel Albright discerned three main tendencies of musical postmodernism: Bricolage (construction or creation of a work from a diverse range of things that happen to be available, or a work constructed using mixed media), Polystylism (use of multiple styles or technique), and Randomness (music in which some element of the composition is left to chance, and/or some primary element of a composed work's realization is left to the determination of its performer(s)). Dylan has no doubt used all these features in his songs, and in his paintings and metal sculptures. Daniel Albright published in the year 2000 two books – *Untwisting the Serpent: Modernism in Music, Literature, and Other Arts* and *Panaesthetics: On the Unity and Diversity of the Art* – where he set a division between arts that try to retain the propriety, the apartness, of their private media, and arts that try to lose themselves in some panaesthetic whole. We will not go further on this topic, but it would be interesting to explore that panaesthetic characteristic regarding Bob Dylan's music.

Most likely Dylan did not go the postmodern route on purpose. He did not wake up one beautiful morning and exclaim: "From now on, I'm gonna make postmodern music!" Nevertheless, he probably knows the postmodern theories, as he was compared to the French artist Marcel Duchamp as recently as 1967. He is conscious of this feature in his work, especially since the 2000s, and it influenced his painting. It showed particularly in the 2012 exhibition *Revisionist Art*, and lately in some of his paintings' titles, and his commentaries in the catalogs that accompanied his exhibition, for they are consciously created and tell stories without caring about the truth. The photographer and painter Richard Prince, well-known as a postmodern artist, sometimes referred to Bob Dylan in his interviews and writings, and some suspect he helped him produce some of his pictorial works, or even he produced them and Dylan just signed them.

After the **Shadow Kingdom** show, the venues opened again, and Bob Dylan went on the road from November 2, 2021 on, allowing us to hear live versions of the songs from his latest album. This tour was announced on the official web site with the name **Rough and Rowdy Ways**, accompanied by the same picture as for "False Prophet," except for a couple dancing in the background, and the dates "2021-2024." There was no explanation on the final date, "2024," so we can only guess it means Dylan will play more or less the same songs until 2024, or else he will stop touring – that I do not believe and do not wish. The accompanying group is a bit different from 2019: guitarist Charlie Sexton is replaced by Doug Lancio, and drummer Charley Drayton took the place of Matt Chamberlain, who replaced George Recile in the last 2019 tour. Bob Britt stays on guitar, Donnie Herron on pedal steel, violin, and others, and of course Tony Garnier on bass.

Bob Dylan wears black jacket and black trousers, sometimes with a bit of grey, and so do the musicians. In the European tour, Dylan wore a different shirt every night, sometimes with ruffles. The stage is lighted from the floor, so that the players appear as silhouettes and we do not see much of their faces. Bob Dylan is center stage, behind the piano. He plays on it all the time, no guitar, and scarce harmonica. He gets up and stays center stage for a few minutes between some of the tracks, and he talks! He introduces the musicians before the last song and says a few sentences each night. In New York, at the Beacon Theater, he said back to a guy in the audience who called for the Woody Guthrie song "Pretty Boy Floyd": "You are in the wrong place, you should go and see Bruce Springsteen on Broadway." And another night, to someone who shouted, "We love you, Bob!" he said back, "There's no Bob here." He jokes by mentioning well-known figures from every town he plays in. In New York, he talked of the Big Apple, of the place where Herman Melville was born, where Jackie Onassis and Sylvester Stallone lived, and in Philadelphia of the Liberty Bell and Frankie Avalon.

The setlist contains seventeen songs and is the same every night. Actually, it varied a bit on the first two nights, they played eighteen songs: "Simple Twist of Fate," replaced the second night by "When I Paint My Masterpiece," as track 5, and "Love Sick" and "It Takes a Lot To Laugh, It Takes a Train to Cry" as encore. From the third night on, the encore was shortened to one song, the same every night, "Every Grain of Sand." The rest of the show[5] contained eight songs from

---

[5] November 5, 2021 setlist: "Watching the River Flow," "Most Likely You Go Your Way (and I'll Go Mine)," "I Contain Multitudes," "False Prophet," "When I Paint My Masterpiece," "Black Rider," "I'll Be

Rough and Rowdy Ways leaving only "Murder Most Foul" and "I Cross the Rubicon."

The versions have more musicality live than in the studio, and most of the time the voice is clear, powerful, and nuanced. The slow tracks especially benefit of sophisticated arrangements, which emphasize their dreamlike quality. It is outstanding in "Key West," where we could hear Donnie Herron's accordion well – on the last tour Dylan changed again this song's arrangements and Herron plays no more accordion. The two songs from the album ***Nashville Skyline***, "I'll Be Your Baby Tonight" and "To Be Alone with You" had their lyrics rewritten, and the latter is much more upbeat. With those two and "Most Likely You Go Your Way," it makes three songs from the 1960s, two from the 1970s – "Watching the River Flow" and "When I Paint My Masterpiece" – two from the 1980s – "Gotta Serve Somebody" and "Every Grain of Sand," and one from 2012, "Early Roman Kings." "I Cross the Rubicon" replaced it since March 3, 2022, making nine songs from ***Rough and Rowdy Ways***. Dylan covers "Melancholy Mood," the only song from the Great American Songbook, replaced in July 2022 by "That Old Black Magic." Both fit well into the show and you could think they were written by himself. "False Prophet" and "Goodbye Jimmy Reed" are among the rocking songs of the show, although the former was a bit slowed down at the end of the 2022 U.S. tour. "Gotta Serve Somebody" was rewritten on the tune of Elvis Presley's "Baby I Don't Care,"

Your Baby Tonight," "My Own Version of You," "To Be Alone with You," "Early Roman Kings," "Key West (Philosopher Pirate)," "Gotta Serve Somebody," "I've Made Up My Mind to Give Myself to You," "Melancholy Mood," "Mother of Muses," "Goodbye Jimmy Reed," "Every Grain of Sand."

and its new lyrics have little to do with religion. Bob Dylan often changed the lyrics in "I Cross the Rubicon," inspired by Homer's Odyssey. "Every Grain of Sand" was replaced by "Friend of the Devil" for a few nights, starting in Oakland, as a tribute to the late Jerry Garcia. Dylan played some guitar in the intro and in the encore for a few nights in the U.S., then he went to Europe and kept to playing the piano.

In Paris (October 12 and 13, 2022), Dylan sang the title line of "I'll Be Your Baby Tonight" half in French, "I'll Be Your Bébé ce soir." In London, the first night, Dylan alluded to John Lennon's comment in 1963, "Is this the place where you're supposed to rattle your jewelry? Is this it? Well rattle your jewelry." On the second night, Bob Britt was absent, Dylan saluted Joe Strummer, whose wife was in the audience. In Nottingham, he played an eighteenth song, "I Can't Seem to Say Goodbye," as a tribute to Jerry Lee Lewis, the "Killer," who died on October 28, 2022. The European tour ended in Dublin, on November 7. After introducing the band after the penultimate song, Dylan said "I want to say hello to Shane MacGowan out there. He's one of our favorite artists and we hope he makes another record soon. 'Fairytale of New York' means a lot to us. We play it every Christmas."

After a seven-year absence, "When I Paint My Masterpiece" reappeared in the setlist on July 27, 2018 and stayed in it so far. In his interview with Douglas Brinkley in 2020, Dylan states this song has grown on him, that it "has something to do with the classical world, something that's out of reach. Something that is so supreme and first rate that you could never come back down from the mountain." The lines:

> Got to hurry on back to my hotel room
> Where I've got me a date with Botticelli's niece

> She promised that she'd be right there with me
> When I paint my masterpiece

were rewritten into:

> Got to hurry on back to my hotel room
> Gonna wash off my clothes,
> scrape off all of the grease
> Gonna lock the doors and
> turn my back on the world for a while
> Gonna stay right there till I paint my masterpiece.

Further on, the narrator adds, "Sometimes I feel like my cup is running over," that alludes (again?) to Psalm 23 in the Bible (cf. **Shadow Kingdom** above), and means he wonders if he reached spiritual abundance. These changes bring a more serious note to the song and transform it into a reflection on the role of the aging artist. What to do when the masterpiece has been painted? Dylan has no intention to rest on his laurels, he continues to compose and goes on tour again, for he cannot stop his quest and must create something different, paint a new masterpiece.

———————————————————

Other Dylan events happened in the 2020s, but they requested little or no involvement of Bob Dylan in person. The release of compilations continued, with the triple CD *Bob Dylan 1970 with Special Guest George Harrison*, the Bootleg Series Volume 16 *Springtime in New York (1980-1985)*, and Volume 17 *FRAGMENTS Time Out of Mind (1966-1997)*, due on January 27, 2023. The latter should be particularly interesting, as it was the beginning of a new phase of creation and inspiration for Bob Dylan, which still expands in the 2020s.

The Bob Dylan Center opened to the public on May 10, 2022. It has 100,000 items, including unseen films and song drafts. It is located in Tulsa, Oklahoma, because it is the home of billionaire philanthropist George Kaiser, and next to the Woody Guthrie Center.

Since May 2022, a metal sculpture by Dylan is permanently exhibited in a wine estate, in the South of France, Chateau La Coste. It is a huge train wagon, named "Rail Car," that may allude to the persecutions of the Jews in the Second World War, and before, since Bob's ancestors were forced to leave their country because of the Jewish pogroms at the beginning of the twentieth century. On a lighter side, it recalls Dylan's long interest in trains. Several exhibitions of his paintings and sculptures took place in various countries. The latest begins on December 16, 2022, at the MAXXI (Museo Nazionale delle Arti del XXI secolo) in Rome. It is entitled *Retrospectrum*, and was shown at Shanghai, Beijing and Miami before.

Bob Dylan recently published an essay titled *The Philosophy of Modern Song*. It was announced in March, and released on November 2, 2022, in the U.S., Britain, France, Germany, The Netherlands, Spain and Italy (Japan coming soon). It contains essays on sixty-six different songs, none by himself. The only Bob Dylan song it mentions is "Subterranean Homesick Blues," apropos of "Pump It Up" by Elvis Costello. The songs' dates range from 1924 (Uncle Dave Macon) to 2004 (Alvin Youngblood Hart), from the twentieth century mainly, only three from the twenty-first century. The style of these comments makes us think of the liner notes for the album "World Gone Wrong." Dylan expresses his impressions of the songs in metaphors, he builds a story from them. It recalls the way Dylan talked on his radio program, *Theme Time Radio Hour* – at the beginning of the book Dylan thanks Eddie Gorodetsky, who lent his music collection for this program – or the things he says to his musicians to explain to them what he wants, how they should play that song he has in mind.

The book has an audio version, spoken by Bob Dylan and a few others. It is a real pleasure for any Dylan fan to hear him read his lines, and the other speakers did a nice job too.

Oddly enough, there is no song by the artists Dylan said at times they were the best, like Woody Guthrie, John Prine, Gordon Lightfoot, Tim Hardin … Neither was there any song by famous artists like The Beatles, The Rolling Stones, Joni Mitchell, Paul Simon, only three by non-American artists. Yet Dylan lists the pop songs with English lyrics based on foreign melodies, including eleven French out of fourteen.

When he says, "bluegrass is the other side of heavy metal," one wonders if it is a wordplay, for this article is about The *Osborne* Brothers, and Ozzy *Osbourne* is a founder of the heavy metal genre, with his group Black Sabbath.

The song "On the Street Where You Live," is mentioned again, as in "Murder Most Foul." The first version of this song was composed supposedly in 2012, and the writing of the book started in 2010, so it is probably no coincidence we found the same song in both. Dylan draws from the same sources of inspiration to write his songs and books (*Chronicles*, and most likely this one, though its sources have not yet been analyzed). He also drew from these sources to make his paintings.

Afterword

The chapter on the "Whiffenpoof Song" by Bing Crosby is another example of Dylan's mischievous mind. This song was written by a vocal group in Yale University, and it is a parody of Rudyard Kipling famous poem, "Gentlemen-Rankers." Moreover, the Whiffenpoofs is a club in Yale, which had for members three generations of the Bush family, both presidents of the United States and Prescott Bush, their father and grandfather. But as noted by the dylanologist Graley Herren, they were also members of a powerful Yale secret society, Skull and Bones. That is why Dylan chose this song, it is obvious when you read the lines: "This song is the grinning skull. [...] a deep dark secret. [...] A lot of bones and skeletons in this song. [...] members of the inner circle." So, is this a convoluted critique on the Bushes and American politics?

Among the 66 songs in the book, Dylan covered many live: "Detroit City," "Money Honey," "Jesse James," "Pancho and Lefty," "You Don't Know Me," "London Calling" (partially), "Blue Suede Shoes" (with Van Morrison), "Key to the Highway," "Big River," "It's All in the Game," "Big Boss Man," and in the studio: "Come Rain or Come Shine," "Your Cheatin' Heart," and "Blue Moon."

The title of the book alludes to Edgar Allan Poe's several essays entitled *The Philosophy of ...*, especially *The Philosophy of Composition*. In this book, Poe explained his theories regarding literature. For him, a written piece should be short, methodical and analytical, not spontaneous, and have a unity of effect. At first examination, Dylan did not follow these rules neither for composing his songs nor for writing his books. But some say Poe himself did not apply those theories for writing his most famous poem, "The Raven," although he took it as an example in this essay. Maybe Dylan gave that name to his book because he thought its content was not serious, just like Poe's essay was not to be taken literally. For Dylan lies, or jests, in his book. First it is no "philosophy," then the songs he chose are not "modern," the "modernest" ones are Elvis Costello's "Pump it Up" and The Clash's "London Calling," which belong to the first new wave after punk. By the way, the Protestant Bible contains 66 books, it shows Dylan still refers to the Scripture, as he did for *Chronicles*, which is the title of the final book of the Hebrew Bible.

As noted by a Philosophy professor of our acquaintance, in *The Philosophy of Modern Song,* we can find similar substance and tone as in the *Theme Time Radio Hour* episodes. On the first level, it is all ironic: it is no treatise on philosophy and the collection of songs is not modern, since most of them date from the 1950s and 1960s, the years when Dylan was young. Even better (or worse?), the most recent recording, "Nelly Was a Lady" by Alvin Youngblood Hart, is actually the oldest one, since it was written in the nineteenth century by Stephen Foster.

On the second level, it is all very serious, contrarywise. If this collection is called "modern," it is on a longer time scale, opposed to the ancient Greek chant. But, even on that scale, Dylan emphasizes more similarity than difference between ancient and modern: it is what he meant by invoking Homer in the Nobel speech, and in the song "Mother of Muses." It is no coincidence either when, in his praise of the American Indian musician John Trudell, he tells us: "There's an ancient spirit coming through him and a person can understand it. His words carry in their simplicity the confidence of ancient wisdom. He's no rapper. More like an *ancient Greek poet*." Ultimately, the deepest way of understanding the term "modern" is to draw away from the mundane chronology and to regard as "modern" the things that were unexpected, whatever the moment in time when they were created. In the part about Elvis Presley, Dylan says tersely: "Art is a disagreement. Money is an agreement." And again, at the end of the article on Trudell: "In a real sense the only thing that truly unites us is suffering and suffering only. We all know loss, whether you're rich or poor. It isn't about wealth or privilege – it's about heart and soul, and there are some people who lack that. They have no landmark on the river's bank to show them how fast they are traveling or where they are heading. And the saddest part is, they will never be able to hear John Trudell."

In the title *Philosophy of Modern Song*, the word "of" does not mean "in," but rather "from." The "modern song" is not any object of study for philosophy, but its living source. The book does not philosophize in any way on the songs – how they are composed, sung, and so on. Instead, it tries something much more difficult and invaluable: bring out from the collection of modern songs of all eras, beyond the sixty-six in the book and the hundreds in *Theme Time Radio Hour*, the philosophy which they are drawn on, in a unique game with time, that is neither adherence to the time that flows, nor the denial of the time in a supposed eternity. The beautiful last – no coincidence – chapter in the book ("Where or When Dion, A Song of Reincarnation") explains the relations between music and time most explicitly: "But so it is with music, it is of a time but also timeless; a thing with which to make memories and the memory itself. Though we seldom consider it, music is built in time as surely as a sculptor or welder works in physical space. Music transcends time by living within it, just as reincarnation allows us to transcend life by living it again and again."

Illustrations, Thanks and Copyrights

Illustrations for this book can be found on the web:

www.bobdylan-fr.com/photos1

www.bobdylan-fr.com/mybooks

Thanks to the following web sites, forums, books, and persons:

Thelma, for her invaluable help with translation and welcome advice

Antoine, who wrote the lines on Philosophy

Joseph, who drew the Bob Dylan portrait on the front page, and kindly offered it to me

John, who edited this book and designed its sleeve

Tim Berners-Lee

bobdylan.com

wikipedia

expectingrain.com/discussions

forums.stevehoffman.tv

rollason.wordpress.com

bob-dylan.org.uk

genius.com

Michael Gray: Bob Dylan Encyclopedia

Michael Gray: Outtakes on Bob Dylan

Oliver Trager: Keys to The Rain, The Definitive Bob Dylan Encyclopedia

Chris Gregory: Determined to Stand – The Reinvention of Bob Dylan

oestrem.com

highsummerstreet.com/2020/07/goodbye-jimmy-reed-hello-van-morrison.html

leadingusabsurd.wordpress.com/2010/03/31/a-portrait-of-bob-dylan-as-the-artist-dylan-and-james-joyce

insidestory.org.au/are-we-there-yet

notesfromtheidiotchild.blogspot.com

dylanology.substack.com

thedylanreview.org

definitelydylan.com

takemeouttraveling.blogspot.com

Graley Herren: The Twilight's Last Gleaming: Dialogues and Debts in Bob Dylan's «Chimes of Freedom»

thedylantantes.substack.com/p/come-you-whiffenpoofs-of-war

All song lyrics written by Bob Dylan, © 2020 for those in the album *Rough and Rowdy Ways*, © 1963 *Long Time Gone*.

www.ingramcontent.com/pod-product-compliance
Lightning Source LLC
Chambersburg PA
CBHW052001090426
42741CB00008B/1494